HITLER

"Marrin writes insightfully about the life of Adolf Hitler and attempts to ascertain the reasons for his fanaticism, as well as the motives of those who blindly followed him. The author forgoes sensationalism, and his matter-of-fact writing style and recitation of events are more than adequate to chronicle the horror. Step-by-step, he describes how Hitler, a seemingly shy, insecure young man was able to inspire a defeated nation that saw the extermination of many of its citizens as its salvation."

—Booklist

"Marrin avoids both psychobabble and outrage as he discusses the childhood influences and failures as a young adult that led to Hitler's destructive, racist personality. . . . A useful, enlightening study of what created Hitler the madman."

—Publishers Weekly

In my will it will one day be written that
nothing is to be engraved on my tombstone
but "Adolf Hitler." I shall create my own
title for myself in my name itself. —ADOLF HITLER

HITLER

ALBERT MARRIN

PUFFIN BOOKS

PUFFIN BOOKS
Published by the Penguin Group
Penguin Books USA Inc., 375 Hudson Street, New York, New York 10014, U.S.A.
Penguin Books Ltd, 27 Wrights Lane, London W8 5TZ, England
Penguin Books Australia Ltd, Ringwood, Victoria, Australia
Penguin Books Canada Ltd, 10 Alcorn Avenue, Toronto, Ontario, Canada M4V 3B2
Penguin Books (N.Z.) Ltd, 182–190 Wairau Road, Auckland 10, New Zealand

Penguin Books Ltd, Registered Offices: Harmondsworth, Middlesex, England

First published in the United States of America by Viking Penguin Inc., 1987
Published in Puffin Books, 1993

1 3 5 7 9 10 8 6 4 2

LIBRARY OF CONGRESS CATALOGING-IN-PUBLICATION DATA
Marrin, Albert.
Hitler / Albert Marrin.   p.   cm.
Originally published: New York: Viking Kestrel, 1987.
Summary: A biography of the struggling Austrian artist who rose from
obscurity to power as the leader of the Nazi party and, later, the
German nation and whose ambitions led the world to war.
ISBN 0-14-036526-5
1. Hitler, Adolf, 1889–1945—Juvenile literature. 2. Heads of
state—Germany—Biography—Juvenile literature. 3. National socialism—
Juvenile literature. 4. Germany—History—1933–1945—Juvenile literature.
[1. Hitler, Adolf, 1889–1945. 2. Heads of state. 3. National socialism.
4. Germany—History—1933–1945.]   I. Title.
DD247.H5M282   1993
943.086'092—dc20   [B]   93-13057   CIP   AC

PHOTOGRAPH CREDITS

Walter Espe, *Das Buch der NSDAP*. Berlin, Schoenfeld's Verlag, 1934:57
The Library of Congress, Washington, D.C.: 10, 11, 50, 169
The National Archives, Washington, D.C.: 27, 63, 70, 76, 80, 82, 103,
121, 125, 142, 152, 190, 194, 202, 212, 229
United States Army: 212, 239
The Wiener Library, London: 95

Maps by Paul Pugliese

Printed in the United States of America

To the memory of the White Rose,
courageous youngsters who spoke the truth
when few others dared.

CONTENTS

PROLOGUE:
THE RIVER OF FIRE

BERLIN, GERMANY, MONDAY, JANUARY 30, 1933. EARLY EVE-
ning, a dull, drizzly Berlin evening.

Crowds had been gathering since morning in the vast
park behind the Brandenburg Gate, a monument crowned
by a statue of the Goddess of Victory driving her war chariot.
At seven o'clock, as darkness settled over the city, tens of
thousands of torches flamed into life. Suddenly a glow visible miles away reflected off the low clouds.

The marchers advanced in dense columns, torches held
high, like an irresistible river of fire. The tramping of jackboots echoed off the buildings lining the street. Men, husky-
voiced and battle-scarred, sang. Their songs were of old
struggles, revenge, and victory.

The fiery river flowed under the Brandenburg Gate and,

3

turning sharply to the right, passed down the broad avenue of the Wilhelmstrasse. All were in uniform, since the marchers had great respect for uniforms and badges of rank. Storm troopers wore brown: brown hats with leather chin straps, brown shirts, brown pants tucked into brown boots. The SS, or Security Service, were clad in black from head to toe, with a silver skull-and-crossbones set above the visors of their caps. Each wore an armband with the colors of their movement: a black swastika set in a white circle against a red field.

Several hundred yards down the Wilhelmstrasse, on the marchers' right, stood the Reich Chancellery, official residence of the head of the German government, the chancellor. Germany had gotten a new chancellor that morning. He stood on the balcony with his aides, gazing on the scene below. Now and then he smiled at the words of a song, especially when storm troopers bellowed:

The rickety bones of the world are shivering with fear,
But to us this fear means a great victory.
For today Germany belongs to us, tomorrow the whole world.

Tomorrow the world! Yes, those were strong words, and he took them seriously.

The chancellor was a man of middle height with straight brown hair and a pale complexion; his only memorable feature was a toothbrush-like mustache. He stood ramrod straight, left hand on his hip, elbow thrust out in a show of defiance. His right arm stretched forward, palm down, in salute to the marchers. They were his men, and they called him *der Fuehrer*—the Leader. As each column passed the balcony, it began a loud chant: *"Heil, Heil, Sieg Heil!*

Heil Hitler!" "Hail, hail, hail victory! Hail Hitler!" No sooner did the chant begin to fade than it was taken up again, louder, by the next column. And so it went for six hours, until the marchers disappeared to their homes, tired but happy.

It all seemed like a miracle, like an impossible dream come true. Adolf Hitler had begun as an unknown soldier from the trenches of the First World War. He'd started with nothing, save an unshakeable faith in himself and his mission. Now, after thirteen years of struggle and disappointment, he'd won. Not only had he built a mighty political party, he'd become head of a nation of eighty million in the heartland of Europe. And this was only the beginning.

Although no one could have known it that night, *der Fuehrer* would dominate Germany for twelve years and three months. During that time he'd wield more power than probably any person in history. His power would reach into the homes of the German people to shape every aspect of their lives. He alone would decide whom they would marry and how they'd raise their children, what music they'd hear and how artists would paint; he even dictated the proper way to cook lobster in restaurants. His word was law, to be obeyed without question on penalty of imprisonment or death. His hatreds and lust for power were boundless. In time his tyranny overflowed the boundaries of Germany to pollute a continent and threaten the entire world. On his orders armies conquered most of Europe, looted its treasures, and enslaved its peoples. At his command millions of innocent people were locked up, starved, tortured, and murdered.

As the fiery river flowed beneath his balcony, *der Fuehrer* was heard to whisper to himself: "No power on earth will ever get me out of here alive." He was right. In the end, everything he'd built crashed in ruins and he met death near this same spot.

Although he caused unimaginable evil, it wasn't because he himself was born evil. People aren't born good or evil. They are born, period. They become good or evil according to how they are shaped by the world and by their life experiences. And so it was with Adolf Hitler. His is a sad, terrible story, and for that reason it must be retold as a lesson to future generations.

YOUNG ADOLF

ADOLF HITLER WAS BORN ON APRIL 20, 1889, IN BRAUNAU, Austria, a small town on the Inn River near the German border. His father, Alois, was an officer in the Austrian customs service, inspecting goods shipped into and out of the country. His mother, Klara, was a peasant girl who'd worked as Alois's maid before their marriage. Alois was nearly twice his wife's age; when they were married in 1885 he was forty-seven, she twenty-four. He'd been married twice before, but both wives had died young, leaving him with a son, Alois, Jr., and a daughter named Angela.

Adolf was born into a family that knew much sadness. His mother had had three children before his birth, each of whom died in infancy. A brother, born when he was five, died after a few years. Only his sister, Paula, who was born when he was seven, outlived him.

Death, however, wasn't the only cause of sadness in the Hitler household. Adolf's parents were as different as day and night. Klara was a gentle, frail person with a pale face and large staring eyes. A model housewife, she cooked, sewed, and kept the home spotless. Although she treated her stepchildren well, her own Adolf was her favorite. He was a sickly baby who she feared might also be taken away. She doted on him, pampered him, catered to his every whim. When he grew older, she constantly told him how special he was, how much better he was than other children. She couldn't say "no" to him. He later called himself his "mother's darling" and used her love to get his own way.

Adolf loved his mother better than any other human being. Throughout his life he carried her picture in his pocket; when he became dictator of Germany, her portrait hung over the head of his bed in each of his homes. He always spoke of her lovingly, tearfully, as the best mother in the world.

It was different with his father. Years later he'd admit, "I never loved my father." Those who knew Alois Hitler agreed that it was difficult to like, let alone love, him. He was a solemn, sour man whose face seemed frozen in a scowl. Cold and distant, lacking any sense of fun, he made every-one around him uncomfortable. Neighbors recalled the feeling of tension that seemed as much a part of his house as its doors and windows. Even when he went out, the house remained filled with his somber presence.

As a government official, Alois wore a uniform with gold braid and carried a pistol. He was a man of authority in the community and he expected to be treated with respect. He demanded silence when he entered a room; no one was allowed to speak unless spoken to. And no one could disagree with him. Joking was forbidden in his presence, and hearty laughter was treated as a crime. Nobody could address him without using his proper title: Senior Customs Inspector. His children had to call him *Herr Vater*—Sir Father.

Yet Alois showed little respect for others' feelings. He had an explosive temper and would fly into a rage for no apparent reason. His shouting was bad enough, but he was also free with his hands. He often beat the children and, when particularly angry, Klara as well.

Little Adolf could never please *Herr Vater*, could never get him to show the smallest sign of love. He called his son as he called his dog, by putting two fingers in his mouth and whistling. He'd slap the child in the face and beat him with a cane, dog whip, or belt. There were times when Adolf, age six or seven, trembled before setting foot in his own home. As much as Klara loved the boy, she didn't dare interfere when Alois went on a rampage.

It soon became clear, however, that Adolf had a mind and a will of his own. The more Alois mistreated him, the more stubborn he became. Adolf liked to read stories about the wars between Indians and settlers in the American West. He favored the Indians, who'd trained themselves to keep silent under torture. One day Alois put him over his knee and beat his backside with a cane. It hurt, but, like an Indian brave, he didn't cry out. This angered his father even more and made him hit harder. At last he gave up, exhausted. From then on, he never whipped his son again. Adolf had won his first battle.

By the time Adolf was nine, the family had moved several times and had finally settled in Leonding, a village near the

Alois Hitler, toward the end of his life.

Klara Hitler, about the time of her marriage.

city of Linz in western Austria. He did well at the local
elementary school. Although he led his classmates in rowdy
games of cowboys and Indians, the teachers liked him. He
was intelligent, studious, and well-behaved in class, earning
excellent grades in every subject.

During this time Adolf broadened his interests and discovered new things about himself. He became fond of poetry
and wrote his own poems in a small leather-covered notebook. When he was twelve, he attended a performance in
the Linz Opera House. The admission wasn't expensive,
just a few pennies for standing room in the balcony. From
then on, he loved music, especially operas about German
legends and heroes. His favorite composer was Richard
Wagner, whose works are still performed in Europe and
America. Adolf saw each of Wagner's operas dozens of
times, becoming so familiar with them that he knew every
note and word by heart.

Adolf also discovered that he could draw. He'd go off by
himself for hours with charcoal and paper. Before long, his
room was cluttered with sketches of buildings and land-
scapes; his scenes are usually without people, as if picturing
humans made him uncomfortable. By the time he entered
his teens, he dreamed of becoming a famous artist.

That dream caused him to rebel against his father. Artists,
Alois yelled, were "not respectable." They were loose, lazy,
dirty people who wasted their lives in poverty. No son of
his would ever become an artist while he lived. Adolf, he
said, must go to the technical school in Linz and become
a civil servant like himself.

That was the last straw. Adolf rebelled at the idea of
spending his life shuffling papers in stuffy offices. Delib-

erately he set out to sabotage his schoolwork, knowing that it would ruin his chances for such a career at the same time as it angered *Herr Vater*.

He began to taunt his teachers, most of whom reminded him of Alois, with smart-aleck questions. He drew nasty pictures of them and spoke of them as "dunces," "dolts," "idiots," "blockheads." Industry gave way to laziness as he worked only at the subjects that interested him. He liked drawing, history, and gymnastics. These he passed. He disliked chemistry, physics, German language, religion, and penmanship. These he failed or passed by the skin of his teeth. The son's failures increased the father's bitterness. He died suddenly in January 1903 at the age of sixty-five.

Although *Herr Vater* couldn't nag him about a civil service career anymore, Adolf's grades didn't improve. In the fall of 1905, he begged his mother to allow him to quit school. At first she hesitated, but he had an answer to her every objection. He insisted that school, with its silly rules and dull teachers, was no place for an artistic person. He could learn much better at home, by himself, he said.

Hitler always remembered the three years after he quit school as the happiest time of his life. Klara made no demands on him and gave him his way in everything. There was no need for him to work. In addition to her widow's pension from the government, she'd sold the house in Leonding and moved to a comfortable apartment in Linz. Alois, Jr., and Angela were grown and on their own, so she could easily support herself and her own children.

Adolf did as he pleased. During the day he roamed Linz with a sketchbook, wrote poetry on a park bench, and visited local libraries. Often he'd spend whole days reading books

on history, mythology, art, and architecture. At night he
went to the theater or the opera. Strangers sometimes mis-
took him for a wealthy gentleman, instead of a dropout
living off his mother. For the opera he wore an elegant suit,
stylish hat, shoes of the finest leather, and carried an ivory-
handled walking stick. Perhaps he enjoyed this lifestyle all
the more, knowing that Alois would have disapproved.

One night at the opera he met August Kubizek, a young
musician who shared his interest in Wagner's works. Kubizek became very important in his life. Since leaving school,
Adolf had become a loner, cutting himself off from boys
his own age; shyness prevented him from speaking to girls.
Kubizek became his friend; indeed, he was the only real
friend he ever had. Years later Kubizek told of their friendship in his book, *The Young Hitler I Knew.*

Being Adolf's friend wasn't always easy. He sulked whenever Kubizek paid attention to other teenagers. "I can't bear
it that you should mix with other young people and talk to
them," he'd say. Mention of getting a job sent him into a
temper tantrum. "Bread-and-butter work" was for "drudges,"
he'd shout, for people like his former schoolmates and his
father. Artistic spirits like himself must be free to explore,
to think, to create. He believed the world owed him a living.
He never held a steady job until he became dictator of
Germany.

Like his father, he insisted upon silence when he spoke.
And, like Alois, he couldn't tolerate disagreement. He only
felt relaxed enough to talk freely around Kubizek. And once
he began to talk, the words tumbled out. He seemed to lose
all self-control. It was as if his ideas and feelings had been
dammed up inside of himself for years. He'd pace about,

shouting and flailing his arms until his voice cracked. Kubizek, who'd listen without comment or interruption, sometimes wondered about his friend's sanity.

Yet Adolf had his likeable side. He was always polite to "Gustl's" parents and brought them small gifts when he visited their home. He was also a sensitive person who could sense when something was troubling his friend. Kubizek recalled:

> Hitler was full of deep understanding and sympathy. He took a most touching interest in me. Without my telling him, he knew exactly what I felt. How often he helped me in difficult times! He always knew what I needed and what I wanted. However intensely he was occupied with himself, he would always have time for the affairs of those people in whom he was interested.

Adolf Hitler at seventeen was clearly a disturbed person, although still able to show kindness and affection. Had things gone differently for him, the world would have been a happier place.

The friends parted company for a while when Adolf went to Vienna in September 1907, to become a full-time art student. It was an emotional farewell at the railroad station. His mother cried and sister Paula sobbed as her big brother boarded the train. Adolf's eyes, too, filled with tears, but he was also happy. At last he was on his way. He had defeated Alois.

Vienna was the capital of Austria-Hungary, a vast empire that dominated Central Europe. Then, as now, Vienna was one of the most beautiful cities on earth. Lying along the

Danube River, it has wide, tree-lined avenues, luxurious palaces, famous museums, and churches with spires soaring heavenward. Music fills the air, from the waltzes in the cafés to the symphonies and operas in the concert halls. After Linz, Vienna was paradise to the enthusiastic youngster.

Adolf rented a room in a respectable boardinghouse and settled down to prepare for the entrance examination to the Academy of Fine Arts. The thought of failure seems never to have entered his mind. The examination, he felt, was a formality; with so much talent, he'd pass easily. Once enrolled in the Academy, he'd do brilliantly, graduate with honors, and become famous in a few years.

But that's not what happened. After going over his work, the judges decided that he had little artistic ability. Their rejection notice struck him like a bolt of lightning. Yet it was only the beginning. A few days later a letter arrived from Linz. His mother needed him. She'd had an operation for cancer and was dying.

Adolf came home with a heavy heart. Although the rejection hurt him deeply, he couldn't burden Klara with his problems. She came first. He did whatever he could to make her comfortable during her last days. Knowing how she liked a clean house, he put on an apron, went down on his knees, and scrubbed the floors. He cooked the meals, always choosing her favorite foods. He slept on a couch near her bed, so as to be near her during the night.

When Kubizek paid his respects, he found his friend calm, but depressed. "Gustl," said Klara when Adolf had stepped out of the room for a moment, "go on being a friend to my son when I am no longer here. He has no one else." She died that evening, December 20, 1907.

Adolf returned to Vienna, where he was joined by Kubizek, who'd been accepted into the Academy of Music. He was determined to succeed this time. Surely, he thought, the rejection had been a mistake. He'd study hard—by himself, of course—and pass with flying colors.

Adolf applied himself as never before. He read art books, sketched, and took private painting lessons for a full year. But despite his efforts, he was rejected again in December 1908. Now began the most terrible time in his life.

No one can succeed in everything, and coping with failure is an essential part of growing up. Most people learn to put failure behind them, overcome the pain, and go on to live happy, productive lives. Unfortunately, the failed art student wasn't such a person. Adolf Hitler had come to Vienna full of hope and enthusiasm. Now, stunned and humiliated, something snapped inside of him. Yes, he'd failed, but he still felt that he had artistic ability. A verse from his favorite opera, Wagner's *Mastersingers of Nuremberg*, spun inside his brain. It gave him no rest, no peace.

> *And still I don't succeed.*
> *I feel it and yet cannot understand it.*

Why had *he* failed? Who was to blame? He didn't know, and not knowing tortured him. Instead of thinking about another career, he dwelled on his failure. He worried it like a half-healed wound, always picking at the scab, never allowing the pain to pass. In his misery Adolf Hitler began to learn things other than art. He learned to hate.

One day, while walking in a rundown section of Vienna, Adolf noticed a man in a black caftan, a long-sleeved gown tied with a sash at the waist, and corkscrew curls dangling behind his ears. The man was a Hasid, Hebrew for "pious person," a member of a group of religious East European Jews. Fascinated, he followed the stranger, studying his features and behavior. He'd never seen anyone like him before. There were Jews in Linz, but, except for their religion, they seemed like everyone else.

His curiosity aroused, he began to read about Jews. Among the things he read were anti-Semitic pamphlets bought from newsstands. Anti-Semitism, hatred of Jews, dates from the Middle Ages in Europe. For centuries Jews were accused of every imaginable crime. Since their religion was different from that of Europe's Christian majority, it was easy to see in them something strange and sinister. Jews were said to have killed Christ, worshipped Satan, and used the blood of murdered Christian children in their ceremonies. Although such charges were rejected by Christian churches in modern times, they were still widespread in Europe early in the twentieth century. People clung to anti-Semitism out of ignorance and because it offered a simple explanation of why things went wrong. If someone had a problem, it was easier to blame "the Jews" than to search for the true cause or face up to one's own responsibility.

The anti-Semitism Hitler read about, however, went even deeper, combining racism with hatred of Jews. Racists believe that there is no such thing as a human family to which we all belong. Although people share the same language and customs, they may actually belong to separate breeds or races. Each race, supposedly, shares a common "blood," which passes its qualities from generation to generation. Thus races are not equal, but arranged in a sort of pyramid with the superior races at the top. The so-called Aryan or Nordic race was represented by the Germans. Aryans were said to be superior to all others, having created everything beautiful and valuable in the world. Negroes, Orientals, and Slavs—Russians, Poles, Czechs—were labeled inferior. Racists believed them cowardly and ignorant, meant by nature to be slaves to their betters.

Jews, racists said, were the most inferior, but also the most dangerous. They wanted to conquer the Aryans through intermarriage, thus poisoning the Aryans' blood and weakening their race. By this means, Jews had become powerful in Austria and other countries. They controlled business, banking, journalism, and the arts. Communism, the idea that industry should be owned by the community instead of wealthy individuals, was a Jewish plot. So was democracy; racists believed only "superior" persons should govern, because ordinary people weren't smart enough to elect able leaders.

Racism is not supported by scientific fact. Anthropologists, students of the world's peoples and cultures, deny that there has ever been a pure race, or that one people is naturally better than others. Germans and Egyptians, Americans and Japanese, are names of nationalities, not races; Slavs speak one of the Slavic family of languages. Similarly, it is as silly to speak of a Jewish race as it is of a Protestant or Muslim race. These are religions held by peoples of many colors, languages, and nationalities.

None of this mattered to young Adolf, whose need to hate outweighed his ability to face facts. Racist anti-Semitism helped him see his own problems in a different light. At last he understood why he'd failed his examinations. It was the Jews! He decided that the Academy officials were secretly Jews who, knowing they lacked his ability, wanted to ruin his career. There was also safety in hating Jews, for then he needn't hate himself for failing.

Once Adolf began to hate, it became harder and harder to stop hating. From the age of nineteen, his hatred deepened, grew stronger, until it passed the bounds of sanity. He had only to hear Jews mentioned, to see them or *think* he saw them, to lose self-control. Hate words spewed from his lips: "rats," "germs," "vermin," "parasites," "bloodsuckers," "maggots." One day, he vowed, he'd get even with them. They'd pay, every last one of them, for the humiliation they'd caused him.

That day, however, was still far in the future. In the meantime, he had to live. Life grew harder as he began to run out of money. He lived frugally, not smoking or drinking, but he never seemed to have enough to meet his needs. He'd go for days on bread and milk to save enough for an opera ticket.

A steady job would have made things easier, but he refused to "lower" himself by working as other men. Instead, he'd wander Vienna muttering to himself about Jews and daydreaming about the future; sometimes he went to a park at night to lecture the trees about his plans. He even set out to write an opera, although he couldn't read music. Nothing ever came of his projects and they were eventually put aside.

One day, when Kubizek returned from visiting his parents, he found the room he shared with Adolf empty. Adolf no longer wished to have a friend, so ashamed was he of his poverty. And so he packed his few belongings and disappeared into the great city without saying goodbye. For the next five years, from the age of nineteen to twenty-four, he lived as a vagrant in Vienna. These years, he'd recall, were "the saddest period of my life."

Vienna, like any large city, was a harsh place for the friendless and poor. Since Adolf refused regular work, he had to take odd jobs in order to live. He shoveled snow, carried luggage outside railroad stations, and beat the dust out of carpets to earn a few coins. When the spirit moved him, he painted small watercolors of Vienna landmarks, which he sold to picture framers or to passersby on the street.

Those who knew him at this time recalled a pitiful figure. His face, thin and pale, was unshaven. From under a greasy black derby hat, his hair hung over his collar. His clothes were threadbare; he once cried when a dealer in old clothes gave him a filthy overcoat that reached to his ankles. The soles of his shoes were full of holes; he often went without socks or underwear.

Where Adolf slept depended on how much money he had. When his pockets were empty, he ate in charity soup kitchens and slept on park benches. In rainy weather, he curled up on the ground under a bridge with his overcoat as a pillow. Winter's cold drove him indoors to the city-run "warming rooms." These were small rooms equipped with a coal stove surrounded by rough wooden tables. The homeless crowded into the rooms at night and, seated on hard benches, fell asleep with their heads on the tables. Warming rooms stank of unwashed bodies and clothes stiff with dirt. The night was filled with sounds of snoring and coughing, and people moaning in their sleep. If he had some money, he rented a cubicle in a shelter for the homeless, where he'd have a bath and sleep in an iron bed on a pillow filled with horsehair.

Young Adolf saw a side of life he'd never imagined. His companions in the warming rooms and shelters were outcasts, loners who'd failed in life. No bonds of brotherhood joined them together. Each looked out for himself or herself, and the devil take the others.

Adolf adapted to this world. Before long, he hated not only Jews, but all of humanity. He became cynical, believing that people act only out of fear and selfishness. Bitterness made him see life as a struggle in which the strong survived at the expense of the weak; he thought it only right that the strong should enslave the weak and kill them when they outlived their usefulness. His world no longer had room for tenderness. To survive, one had to be like a jungle beast: hard, cunning, cruel. All this the frustrated artist learned in Vienna, "the hardest, most thorough school of my life."

In May 1913 Adolf left this place of suffering for Munich, a city in the South German state of Bavaria. He'd been thinking of making this move for a long time. As an anti-Semite and racist, he believed that his homeland was too corrupt to be saved. He saw Germany as the Aryans' last stronghold, a haven for people like himself. Besides, at twenty-four he was three years overdue in registering for military service. The thought of serving in Austria's army made him angrier than usual. Not that he was a coward—far from it. But he had no intention of mixing with Jews and other "inferiors" in the army.

Arriving in Munich, Hitler rented a room over a tailor-shop near the university, in a section still favored by artists.

There he set up his easel and painted watercolors, which he sold in beer gardens, outdoor taverns where people drank tall tankards of beer and ate thick sausages with sauerkraut. Sometimes he joined the customers' discussions, only to have a temper tantrum if anyone disagreed with him.

Mostly, however, he kept to himself. Neighbors found him polite enough, although he seemed unsure about what to do with his life. He had no friends, no home, no career, and, apparently, no future.

All of that changed when the First World War began in the summer of 1914. There is a snapshot taken on August 2 of a crowd gathered in Munich's Odeon Square to hear the reading of the declaration of war against Russia and France; Germany, Great Britain, and Belgium would go to war a few days later. Hitler's face can be seen in the midst of the cheering crowd. Wide-eyed, his lips parted, he seems overjoyed. In fact, the coming of war was his happiest moment in years. "For me," he'd recall, "those hours came as a deliverance from the distress that weighed upon me during the days of my youth. I am not ashamed to admit that I was carried away with enthusiasm. I fell on my knees and thanked Heaven from the fullness of my heart that it had granted me the favor of being allowed to live in these times."

The next day, he volunteered for the German army and was accepted into the List Regiment, an infantry outfit named for its commander, Colonel Wilhelm List. Although Austria-Hungary and Germany fought on the same side, and he was still an Austrian citizen, he considered himself a German.

Hitler had reason to be pleased with himself. The war

that would kill and maim millions of young men came as
a blessing to the twenty-five-year-old dropout. It offered him
a fresh start in life. His private's uniform showed that he
was a member of a powerful organization whose glory he
shared. For the first time since leaving home, he felt at
peace with himself. Now that he was a warrior of the German Empire, his duty was not to think for himself, but to
obey orders.

After basic training, the List Regiment was sent to the
Western Front to fight the British and Belgians. The future
warlord's baptism of fire came in October 1914, at Ypres,
Belgium. His company was advancing through a morning
fog when high-explosive shells began dropping all around.
Hitler described the scene in a letter to an acquaintance in
Munich:

> . . . the first [shell] hisses over us and explodes at
> the edge of the forest, splintering the trees as if they
> were straws. We watch with curiosity. We have no
> idea as yet of the danger. None of us is afraid. Every-
> one is waiting impatiently for the command, "For-
> ward!" . . . We crawl on our stomachs to the edge
> of the forest. Above us are howls and hisses, splin-
> tered trees and branches surround us. Then again
> shells explode at the edge of the forest and hurl
> clouds of stones, earth and sand into the air, tear
> the heaviest trees out by their roots, and choke every-
> thing in a yellow-green terribly stinking steam. . . .
> Four times we advance and have to go back; from
> my whole batch one remains, besides me, [and]
> finally he also falls. A shot tears off my right coat

sleeve, but like a miracle I remain safe and alive.
At two o'clock we finally . . . occupy the edge of
the forest and farms.

At first the Germans advanced steadily. They overran
Belgium's major cities and, turning south, headed for Paris,
the French capital. Only desperate fighting and hundreds
of thousands of casualties brought them to a standstill. By
Christmas 1914 the war seemed to go into slow motion,
with neither side able to strike the knockout blow. The
opponents dug lines of trenches extending for five hundred
miles from the border of Switzerland to the North Sea.
These hellholes of mud and blood became graves for millions of men.

During the next four years Hitler fought in forty-seven
battles, among them some of the most terrible of the war.
He was at Messines Ridge, Belgium, when the List Regiment was nearly wiped out; of the three thousand who went
into action, fewer than five hundred were able to walk away
under their own power. The others were killed, wounded,
or disappeared without a trace; anyone caught in the explosion of a large-caliber shell vanished, leaving behind
nothing more than a few bloody rags and lumps of flesh.
Hitler also took part in the Battle of the Somme in northern
France. It was a bloodbath. For three months the British
drenched the German lines with explosives in order to break
through to the open country beyond. But the Germans held
on, costing the enemy twenty thousand dead in the first
day's fighting; the British suffered 614,000 casualties by the
end of the battle.

Hitler became used to the sights and sounds of war. For

weeks on end, he lived with the chatter of machine-gun fire and the crack of rifle bullets in his ears. The roar of enemy shells was followed by shock waves, and domes of earth heaved skyward. The air hummed with shell splinters, each able to slice through a man like a buzz saw. Dead men and parts of dead men lay everywhere, rotting and stinking. The wounded might lie for days in the barbed-wire entanglements in front of the trenches, screaming and whimpering until, one by one, they fell silent. It was foolish to risk more lives to rescue the wounded or bring in the dead for burial.

Unlike most soldiers, who loathed the slaughter and wished only to get home in one piece, Hitler enjoyed the war. As far as he was concerned, it could have continued forever. He never complained, never tried to play sick, never wanted to be anywhere else but in the trenches.

Although the men of his company thought him strange, they respected him as a soldier. He was a good soldier. Danger didn't faze him; indeed he volunteered for danger-ous assignments. The wounded knew that Adolf at least would take any risk to bring them to safety.

Hitler led a charmed life, always escaping harm as if a higher power protected him. Men might be dropping every-where, but he'd come through without a scratch. He had a feeling about danger, which he couldn't explain but which saved his life several times. Once, while eating dinner in a trench with some comrades, he heard a voice in his head, which said, "Get up and go over there." He stood up and, without another word, walked twenty yards down the trench with his mess kit in his hand. He'd just sat down to continue eating when a flash and a *bang* came from the spot he'd

Hitler, seated on left, with some of his comrades on the Western Front, around 1916.

just left. A stray shell had landed in the group, killing everyone.

Hitler's courage and luck were noticed by his superiors, who promoted him to corporal and made him a dispatch runner. Before radios enabled commanders to keep in touch with frontline troops, messages had to be carried by runners. Dispatch running was dangerous work, and most were killed or crippled within a few weeks.

Not Corporal Hitler. When shellfire raked the trenches and snipers shot anyone who raised his head, he'd leap from cover and run with his message. He was so good at his job, and liked it so much, that he'd ask others to allow him to carry their messages as well as his own.

Hitler won six medals for bravery, including the Iron Cross, the German version of our Medal of Honor. The reward was all the more precious, because it was rarely given to common soldiers. Hitler is supposed to have earned the Iron Cross for capturing singlehandedly fifteen enemy soldiers while acting as a dispatch runner.

Hitler was wounded twice during his exploits. A shell splinter flew into his face, hurting him slightly, during the Battle of the Somme, October 1916. A few days later, a shell fragment struck his left leg. This time the doctors put him on a hospital train and sent him to Germany for treatment.

Soldiers prayed for a wound like Hitler's. Though serious, it wasn't crippling or life-threatening. It was just the thing to get you out of the trenches honorably for a few weeks of rest and good food in a hospital. Hitler, however, was restless in the hospital, especially when he heard the complaints of fellow patients. These men were disgusted with the war; the slaughter had gone on for too long, they said. They wanted peace, even if Germany had to give up territory she'd taken. Such talk annoyed Hitler, who asked to be sent back to the front as soon as he could walk. He was more comfortable there than anywhere else.

Not that his comrades were comfortable with him. Far from it. Always a loner, he never laughed, joked, or griped as soldiers have done through the ages. He'd sit in the corner of a trench, his head in his hands, brooding. Suddenly he'd leap up, shouting racist slogans he'd learned in Vienna.

Some of his habits were also strange. He was fascinated with the trench rats, red-eyed creatures grown fat on un-buried bodies. While others tried to sleep, Hitler sat in the darkness without moving a muscle. When he heard rats scurrying, he turned on his flashlight and spitted them on his bayonet. He kept this up until a hail of rocks and curses made him stop.

On October 14, 1918, Hitler was in a trench when the whine of gas alarms sounded in the distance. Silently a mustardy-brown cloud of poison gas drifted over the German positions from the British lines. The gas found an opening in his mask, around the goggles. It felt as if someone had passed a red-hot poker across his eyes. Within minutes he was blind.

The doctors sent him to an army hospital near Berlin. He'd been lucky that the gas hadn't gotten into his lungs, they said; then his face would have turned purple as he slowly choked to death. Still, it was bad enough. He lay in bed for weeks with his eyes swathed in bandages. He lay in blackness, terrified that his sight might never return.

On November 10, 1918, the patients well enough to

move were brought into the hospital's main hall. A pastor, an elderly man, grave and gray-haired, stood before them. A lot had happened since they'd been wounded, he said. Revolutionaries had seized control, or were battling police, in Germany's major cities. Kaiser Wilhelm II, the emperor, had resigned his throne and fled to Holland. A republic had been declared in Berlin. An armistice, or cease-fire, would go into effect on all fronts the next morning. The pastor bowed his head and, sobbing, finished his announcement. The German army must surrender to the Allies. The war was over.

A stunned Adolf Hitler groped his way back to his room and threw himself on the bed. Burying his head in the pillow, he cried for the first time since his mother's death. His tears were for Germany, but also for himself. The army had given his life purpose and meaning; a uniform and medals made him *somebody*. But what would become of him now that it was defeated? He couldn't bear the thought of returning to Munich as a nobody—a blind nobody.

The days and nights that followed were agony for him. He lay awake, brooding about the disaster. His feverish mind raced. Voices called to him. Ideas popped into his mind as if they weren't part of himself, but had a life of their own.

Somehow he decided that he and Germany were alike. Just as he'd failed in Vienna through no fault of his own, Germany hadn't been defeated on the battlefield. No! She'd been betrayed and her army "stabbed in the back" by the same people who'd ruined his artistic career. "Wretched and miserable criminals," he called them, remembering his anger years later. "In those nights my hatred arose, the hatred against those responsible for this deed."

Adolf Hitler—dropout, failure, blinded soldier—convinced himself that God had chosen him for a mission. That's why his life had been spared when so many others died. He would right Germany's wrongs, rebuild her armies, and punish the traitors. At last he knew who he was and what he had to do. "I decided to become a politician."

Seldom has one person's decision been filled with so much danger for humanity.

THE PATH TO
POWER

THE "TRAITORS" CORPORAL HITLER VOWED TO PUNISH WERE
actually millions of ordinary Germans made desperate by
the hardships of war. Germany in the fall of 1918 was a
land of misery. Although she'd been spared fighting on her
soil, the war effort had drained her resources. Basic metals,
chemicals, and medicines were unavailable; coal, needed
to power factories and heat homes, was scarce. For lack of
cloth, newborn babies were wrapped in rags and hospitals
used bandages made of paper and cotton. Four years of the
Allied blockade had cut off supplies of imported food, vital
even in peacetime, for Germany never grew enough to feed
her entire population. As a result, the main food became
bread made up of turnips and "edible" sawdust, plus rotten
cabbages and potatoes.

Living skeletons roamed the streets of Germany's cities, looking for dead horses and fighting over a handful of putrid flesh. Starvation claimed hundreds each day. Often there was no wood for coffins and people were buried in mass graves; small children were laid to rest in cardboard boxes.

These conditions destroyed the people's will to continue the war. Many looked to Russia, where Communists had toppled the government in 1917 and taken the country out of the war. Communists, or Marxists, were followers of Karl Marx, a nineteenth-century German economist who wanted to improve workers' living conditions. Marx preached world revolution. He wanted existing governments overthrown and replaced by Communist dictatorships. All banks, businesses, stores, factories, mines, and farms were to be taken from their owners and put under ownership of the new Communist governments. That's what happened when the Communist Party took over in Russia, renamed the Soviet Union. Under V. I. Lenin and Joseph Stalin, all other political parties were abolished and opponents were eliminated by firing squads.

German Communists, joined by ordinary people, most of whom only wanted food, revolted. Troops sent to keep order frequently joined the rebels; the sailors of the German High Seas Fleet mutinied. As Hitler lay blinded, the emperor fled and rebels seized Berlin, Munich, and other cities, forcing an end to the war.

Hitler regained his eyesight in the weeks following the Armistice and returned to his regiment, now stationed outside Munich. His immediate problem was not getting into politics, but living from day to day. Germany's armed forces were being disbanded in keeping with the terms of surrender.

All warships, planes, tanks, and big guns were to be turned over to the Allies or destroyed. Only several thousand troops equipped with small arms—pistols, rifles, light machine guns—were allowed to remain on duty. Hitler, too, would have been discharged had he not deserved special treatment as a winner of the Iron Cross. His superiors kept him on to guard French prisoners awaiting release and to sort mountains of used equipment. For the time being, he had food, clothing, and a roof over his head.

Meanwhile elections were held for a national assembly to draw up a constitution for Germany. Since Berlin was occupied by rebels, the assembly met in the city of Weimar. The republic received its constitution there, which is why we call it the Weimar Republic.

The Weimar Republic was a democracy with a freely elected *Reichstag*, or parliament, which made the laws. A president, also elected, appointed the chancellor, who headed the cabinet and was leader of the party with the largest number of delegates in the Reichstag. The chancellor and cabinet saw that the laws were carried out and ran the country on a daily basis. As with our Bill of Rights, civil liberties such as freedom of speech and religion were guaranteed by the constitution.

The early days of the Weimar Republic were stormy. First, it had to govern a ruined nation with rebels holding the major cities. It had also to meet with the Allies to work out a treaty ending the war. Neither task was pleasant or easy.

With the army disbanding, the government took any help it could get to crush the rebellion. Soon billboards were plastered with posters calling upon veterans to join armed units called *Freikorps*—Free Corps. The posters appealed to the veterans' patriotism and fear of Communists, who were shown as beasts destroying the German nation.

Volunteers, frontline soldiers with scores to settle, came in the thousands from every corner of Germany. For them, as for Hitler, war had become a way of life. They'd learned in the trenches that human life is cheap and killing is all right, as long as it's done in a "good cause." Like Hitler, they couldn't accept defeat. They hated the rebels, believing they had stabbed the army in the back.

Artillery and tanks weren't necessary for what they set out to do; small arms and bayonets were enough. During the early months of 1919, Free Corps units stormed the rebel strongholds and took their revenge. *"An die Wand, Schweinehund"*—"Up against the wall, dirty dog"—became their battle cry. Thousands of people, rebels as well as innocent bystanders, were shot without trial. The Free Corps had brought the war from the trenches into the streets of their homeland.

Although they saved the Weimar Republic, the Free Corps hated it as much as the rebels they killed. They never forgave its leaders for signing the Treaty of Versailles in June 1919.

The peace conference ending the First World War met at the Palace of Versailles outside Paris. There the Allies—Great Britain, France, Belgium, and Italy—forced the Republic's delegates to accept a treaty most Germans felt to be unjust. Germany had to take full blame for starting the war. Large chunks of her territory were given to Poland and Czechoslovakia, together with their German-speaking inhabitants; Alsace-Lorraine, taken from France in an earlier war, was returned. In addition to losing her colonies in

Africa and the Pacific, Germany was to pay for all damage suffered by the Allies during the war. Her armed forces, once the strongest on earth, were crippled. The army was limited to one hundred thousand men, the navy to a fraction of that number. Germany was forbidden to build weapons of "attack": tanks, submarines, military aircraft, heavy warships.

News of the treaty brought demonstrations throughout Germany. Free Corps members, but also millions of people who'd never fired a gun, denounced the treaty and the government that accepted it. Both the revolutionaries and the Weimar Republic were accused of betraying the nation. In the years that followed, ex–Free Corps soldiers assassinated several of the leaders who'd signed the treaty.

In September 1919, three months after the Treaty of Versailles went into effect, Adolf Hitler took his first steps along the path to power. He took them, not of his own free will, but because he was pushed.

Officers in the Munich command needed a man to spy on political groups suspected of "disloyalty"—that is, of disagreeing with the military. Already Germany's defeated generals were thinking of rearmament and wanted to keep tabs on those who might oppose them. Hitler, with his towering hatred of Jews and "traitors," was just the man they needed.

One day he attended a meeting of about twenty-five people in the back room of a cheap Munich tavern. The room, dimly lit and stuffy, smelled of stale beer and cigars. The group called itself the German Workers' Party, but was more like a debating club than a political party. Founded by

Anton Drexler, a mechanic in the railroad yards, it met to discuss ways of creating a better Germany. Although everyone agreed that Jews and Marxists were to blame for the country's problems, the party had no plan or program to set things right.

Hitler was unimpressed and said so in his report. He was all the more surprised when, a few days later, the mail brought his membership card in the German Workers' Party. He was party member 555; but since the numbering began at 500, the party had only fifty-five members. They had given him this "honor" without his permission. Hitler didn't know whether to laugh or be angry until his superiors decided for him.

His report had found its way to General Erich von Ludendorff, former commander of German forces on the Western Front. Ludendorff, eager to support groups friendly to the army, ordered Hitler's superiors to have him join the German Workers' Party and help it grow.

Hitler began attending meetings and participating in discussions. Something curious happened, which he hadn't suspected about himself. He realized that he could speak in public. The boy who'd unburdened himself to Kubizek was gone. So was the young drifter, who seldom spoke to people, and then only to argue and hurl insults. Now a man of thirty-one, he found people who agreed with him. More than that: the more he spoke, the more enthusiastic they became and the more control he had over them. Speech, he discovered, was not only a means of communication, but an instrument of power.

Hitler took every opportunity to speak in public. He spoke at street corners, on railroad platforms, in parks—anywhere people passed in large numbers. He spoke in all weather, even snowstorms, without a microphone.

Few paused to listen at first. But in time scores, then hundreds, gathered around him. When the crowds became too large, he rented beer halls, then a circus theater. He distributed handbills advertising his speeches. As many as six thousand people came to hear him give such talks as "The Jews are our misfortune," "Germany awake!" and "Versailles, Germany's destruction."

Once Hitler discovered his power over crowds, he began to work as never before. The work was hard, the hours long, but he was driven by a burning ambition. Material rewards didn't interest him; they'd come later. He worked to mold the German Workers' Party into a weapon that would make him dictator of Germany. Then, he promised, "heads will roll."

There was plenty to do. When he joined the party, its treasury, kept in a cigar box, totaled seven marks ($2.25). It had no newspaper, no pamphlets, no offices; there wasn't even a rubber stamp. Announcements were prepared on a portable typewriter rented from a party member.

This ended once Hitler was put in charge of propaganda. Although he resigned from the army soon after joining the party, he still kept in touch with its intelligence department. His contacts there gave him money from secret army funds to buy a daily newspaper, *The People's Observer*. They also introduced him to members of the Bavarian state government, who might be helpful if he overstepped the law.

Hitler, the failed artist, proved to be a master propagandist who knew how to win people's minds. One of his cleverest moves was to take the hooked cross, or swastika, as the party's emblem. The swastika is an ancient symbol of good luck signifying the passage of the sun across the sky. Swastikas are found in the art of many peoples. Persians carved them into temple walls; American Indians painted them on clothing and tipis. Under Hitler, the swastika stood for anti-Semitism and the "purity" of the Aryan race. A bold, eye-catching design, it could easily be painted on walls or chalked on sidewalks. Hitler used it on everything: armbands, lapel buttons, stationery, helmets, cuff links, tie pins, signet rings. Cardboard swastikas were tossed from speeding cars or rooftops, and drifted downward like pinwheels. The flag he designed, a black swastika in a white circle on a red field, was filled with menace. Hundreds of these flags and banners whipping in the wind resembled streaming blood.

In April 1920, Hitler changed the party's name to National Socialist German Workers' Party, or Nazi Party for short. "Nazi" is a shortening of the first word of the German name: NAtionalsoZIalistische. Early the next year, Hitler was recognized as chief of the Nazi Party. He gave himself the title *Fuehrer*, Leader.

Yet the source of Hitler's growing influence remained his ability as a speaker. No speaker in modern times could match his talent for winning over masses of people. Years later, when Germany lay in ruins, many wondered why they'd been carried away by his speeches. It was as if they'd been hypnotized by a magician, an evil genius with supernatural powers.

Hitler never read his speeches from a prepared text; at most, he scribbled some key words on a sheet of paper. He'd enter a hall amid blaring bands and cheers of *"Heil*

Hitler" and walk alone to the speaker's platform. The crowd fell silent, waiting breathlessly for his words. At first they came haltingly in a rough, raspy voice. After a few sentences, he might stop for minutes at a time, as if puzzled and unsure of himself. Actually, his fumbling was like an insect's feeling about with its antennae. Hitler was getting the "feel" of the crowd, sensing its members' resentments and hidden hurts. Once he grasped these, he cut loose with an explosion of verbal fury.

Logic and truth had no place in his speeches. Hitler had no respect for truth. Lies and trickery, he believed, were stronger than truth and therefore were good in themselves. He'd boast to Nazi lieutenants that they'd never know when he was telling the truth or lying. He lied for the fun of deceiving others and to spread confusion, thus keeping his enemies off balance.

His speeches were exercises in what he called the Big Lie. Hitler thought that most people, even most Aryans, were "stupid," "lazy," and swayed mainly by their emotions. To win them over, therefore, it was necessary to stir their emotions with lies. If he lied long enough and strong enough, he thought people would believe anything, no matter how ridiculous it sounded.

In order to excite others' emotions, Hitler had to whip himself into a frenzy. As he spoke, his face flushed and the veins stood out in his neck. Fists clenched and unclenched, screaming at the top of his voice, he spat out his hatred. Violent words—"smash," "hate," "fight," "crush"—gushed from his lips in an uncontrollable flood. Flecks of foam glistened in the corners of his mouth, and his hair, dripping with sweat, hung limply on his forehead. Speaking was so strenuous that he'd lose as much as five pounds in an evening.

Hitler's emotion ignited the emotions of the crowd. People lost control of themselves, trembling, sobbing, weeping, howling. Men as well as women fainted or rolled in the aisles. They were bewitched.

When he'd brought them to a feverish pitch, Hitler suddenly stopped and strode from the hall, leaving them breathless and eager to tell others of their experience. Kurt Leudecke, an early follower, described how he surrendered to Hitler during a speech: "His words were like the lashes of a whip. When he spoke of Germany's disgrace, I was ready to spring on my enemy. . . . The intense will of the man, the passion of his sincerity, seemed to flow from him into me. . . . It was just like a religion. . . . I gave him my soul."

One of Hitler's best allies turned out to be that same Weimar Republic he'd sworn to destroy. Early in 1923, the government, unable to pay its bills, began to print money without gold or silver backing. The result was *inflation*— that is, increasing the money supply so that its value is lowered and prices rise. When the war began in 1914, four German marks equaled one American dollar. In January 1923, it took 17,792 marks to equal that same dollar. By year's end, there were 4,200,000,000,000 (four trillion two hundred billion) marks to the dollar.

It was a disaster. Prices skyrocketed. Eggs cost a million marks apiece. Housewives took suitcases full of money to buy a loaf of bread. If a bundle of bills fell into the gutter, it wasn't worth stopping to pick up. Workers were paid twice a day, with time off to go shopping before prices soared still higher. There was so much money around, and it was worth so little, that the colorful bills were used as wallpaper.

Most Germans suffered from the inflation. With food scarce, workers never seemed to earn enough to make ends meet. Anyone with a bank account saw the value of his savings melt away. The aged, who depended on savings and pensions, were rewarded with poverty for lifetimes of thrift. Inflation benefited only those who owed money. The government, which had to repay war loans, and businessmen, who'd borrowed to expand factories to profit from the war, settled their debts easily. Thus if you owed a million marks in 1914, it was worth $250,000. With such high inflation, you could cancel the debt for less than a penny.

Inflation drew people to Hitler like a magnet. Thousands who suffered through no fault of their own flocked to hear his raging speeches. He gave words to their feelings, releasing their pent-up anger. If they wondered why they suffered so terribly, he gave them the answer. It was a short, simple answer anyone could understand: The Jews and their puppets, the Communists and the Weimar Republic, were responsible for everything. People listened and, in their confusion and pain, fell for the Big Lie.

Hitler also attracted haters, misfits, and bullies, some of whom would rise to power with their master. Dangerous men, they had no respect for God, or law, or decency.

There was Julius Streicher, a squat, bull-necked ex-schoolteacher who always carried a whip. Streicher owned *The Stormer*, a newspaper filled with obscene attacks on the Jews.

Ernst Roehm, ex-soldier and Free Corps fighter, enjoyed violence for its own sake. "Since I am an immature and wicked man," Roehm boasted, "war and unrest appeal to me more than order."

Rudolf Hess, an anti-Semite and veteran of the List Regiment, became Hitler's secretary. Hess worshipped his leader and followed him like a faithful puppydog. "*Mein Fuehrer,*" he'd cry, "you are Germany!" Or again: "With pride we see that one man remains beyond criticism. This is because everyone feels and knows that Hitler is always right, and that he will always be right."

Hermann Goering had led the famous Flying Circus fighter squadron during the war, downing twenty-two Allied planes. A fat, happy-go-lucky fellow, he laughed heartily, drank deeply, and was a drug addict. He liked gaudy clothes and wore lipstick and rouge at private parties. Goering worshipped Hitler; sometimes he'd spring to attention when the Fuehrer called on the telephone. He knew no right or wrong, except what Hitler ordered. His motto was: "I have no conscience! Adolf Hitler is my conscience!" One day Goering would lead the *Luftwaffe*, the reborn German airforce.

Veterans, including thousands of ex-Free Corps fighters, flocked to the swastika banner. Hitler formed them into the *Sturmabteilung*, storm troopers, named for the crack troops that had spearheaded German attacks on the Western Front. The storm troopers were Hitler's bullyboys, a private army sworn to obey him without question. Their job was to protect Nazi rallies and disrupt opponents' meetings, especially the Communists'. Although the Communist revolutionaries had been defeated, Germany still had a large Communist Party with its own strongarm squads. Whenever Nazis and Communists met, fists, and sometimes bullets, flew.

The storm troopers' first real action was the Battle of the

Beer Hall, November 4, 1921. Hitler knew that Communists wanted to ruin his speech at one of Munich's largest
beer halls. Before the meeting, he gave a pep talk to his
fifty-man unit, ordering them to attack at the slightest sign
of trouble. The men clicked their heels, shouted "*Heil Hitler!*" and went oft singing a fighting song.

That night 2,200 people gathered in the hall. Much to
the Nazis' surprise, 700 were Communists, and they were
spoiling for a fight.

Hitler stood on a table and began his usual speech. The
Communists, unimpressed, began to heckle. Hitler noticed
them ordering lots of beer and hiding the empty mugs, heavy
glass containers, under the tables. They were collecting
ammunition.

Suddenly a big, beefy man with a red neck leaped on a
table and shouted "*Freiheit!*"—"Freedom!"—the signal to
attack. Instantly scores of beer mugs flew at Hitler's head.
He stood his ground, calling for his men to go into action;
he'd dodged worse than beer mugs in the trenches.

The outnumbered storm troopers plowed into the audience. It was a grand brawl. Men grabbed beer mugs by the
handle, smashed them, and used the jagged edges as brass
knuckles. Chairs flew. Tables were torn apart and the legs
used as clubs. The battle raged for twenty minutes, until
the storm troopers, bloody but unbeaten, threw the Communists out of the hall. Then the voice of a Hitler follower
boomed, "The meeting continues. The speaker has the
floor."

Instead of driving people away from the Nazis, violence
made them seem adventurous, attracting more members.
By the summer of 1923, the Party had 35,000 members in

Munich and 150,000 in the whole of Bavaria. Of these, 11,000 were storm troopers.

Goering and Roehm welded these roughnecks into a disciplined force. They wore brown uniforms, thick belts, and jackboots. When they fought, they donned steel helmets, gifts from friendly army officers. The storm troopers could often be seen, as many as 6,000 strong, parading through Munich, singing:

> *Swastika on helmet*
> *Armband black-white-red,*
> *Storm Detachment Hitler*
> *Is our name.*

They marched unarmed, although everyone knew they could easily put their hands on guns. *Der Fuehrer* had gathered stockpiles of small arms and hidden them "just in case."

Hitler's ambition grew as Nazi numbers increased. In November 1923 he decided the time was right for a *Putsch*, or armed revolt. His plan was to take control of the Bavarian state government and with its support march to Berlin to overthrow the republic. Neither the army nor the Bavarian State Police would interfere, for their leaders also hated the republic; if anything, they'd join him, he believed.

On the evening of November 8, 1923, supporters of the Bavarian government held a rally in the Buergerbrau Keller, another large Munich beer hall. Bavarian State Commissioner Gustav von Kahr was speaking when armed storm troopers surrounded the building. Hitler, in the meantime, slipped inside unnoticed with some of his henchmen; Kahr had been droning on for a half hour and many in the audience were drowsy with boredom and beer.

Der Fuehrer drew a revolver and raced down the aisle, firing two shots into the ceiling. *That* got the audience's attention. He leaped on the speaker's platform and glared at the audience. "The national revolution has begun," he shouted, waving his gun. No one must leave the hall. Unless everyone obeyed, he'd have storm troopers place machine guns in the balconies above.

As his grim-faced men stood guard, Hitler hustled the three most powerful men in Bavaria into a back room: Kahr, General Otto von Lossow, commander of the army troops in Bavaria, and Colonel Hans Ritter von Seisser, chief of the Bavarian State Police. Hitler waved his revolver under their noses and shouted. He had four bullets left. If they didn't join him, he promised to shoot them and then commit suicide.

Although Hitler's prisoners had little respect for the republic, they had none for him. They were aristocrats, noblemen; he was a hysterical ex-corporal. "*Nein!*" No! They'd never help him.

Just then General Ludendorff arrived, brought from home by a squad of storm troopers. He was furious at Hitler for staging a putsch without telling him, and in a beer hall at that! Nevertheless Ludendorff agreed to support the revolt. He barked some commands and the prisoners agreed to join in. With that settled, they were freed and the audience was allowed to go home.

The Nazis had blundered. Kahr and his companions thought Hitler a lunatic and would have said anything to get away from him. Once free, however, they meant to stamp out his rebellion. The Munich garrison was alerted;

police armed with rifles and machine guns were ordered into the streets.

For once Hitler lost his nerve. Everything had gone wrong. He had planned his putsch with the help of the army and police, not against them. When he learned of Kahr's "betrayal," he wanted to send the storm troopers into hiding and flee himself.

Ludendorff disagreed. If Hitler hadn't the courage to finish what he'd begun, the general would lead the storm troopers in a bid to take over Munich. Millions of men had once obeyed Ludendorff's orders, including many who were now supposed to be against the Nazis. They wouldn't dare fire on him. When ex-Corporal Hitler objected, he cut him off. "*Wir marschieren!*"—"We shall march!"—he snapped.

And march they did. The next afternoon, November 9, three thousand singing, chanting storm troopers set out for the center of Munich. They marched in old army battle-dress—helmets, packs, web belts—and carried rifles. At their head were Hitler wearing his Iron Cross, Ludendorff, Goering, Streicher, among others. The flag bearer was a thin, spectacled youth named Heinrich Himmler. As they marched, thousands of onlookers lined the way to cheer them on. Thousands more swung into line behind the column. The Nazis had plenty of support from the people of Munich.

All went well until they neared the entrance to Odeon Square, where a hundred police barred the way. Although greatly outnumbered, the police held their ground, staring down their rifle barrels at the Nazis.

Time stood still, as both sides eyed each other. The only sound was the wind and the patter of large, wet snowflakes.

Crack!

Nobody knows who fired the first shot, but it was followed by a hail of lead from both sides. When the smoke cleared, sixteen Nazis and three policemen were sprawled lifeless in the street. Wounded lay everywhere, moaning or thrashing in pain.

Hitler, the former dispatch runner, instinctively dropped to the ground at the first shot. He remembered the spot, almost exactly where he'd stood to cheer the war in August 1914. Except for a dislocated shoulder, he was unhurt.

Only Ludendorff kept going. With bullets whipping past him, he marched up to the police, ramrod straight, chin up. The officers, awed by the famous commander, parted ranks to let him through. Moments later, a lieutenant placed him under arrest. Glaring at his captors, he spat out an insult, "You are all revolting. I want to vomit before you."

No Nazis followed Ludendorff. They scattered (those who could) to the four winds. Some went into hiding. Others fled the country. A few were arrested. After hiding out for a few days, Hitler surrendered to the police while shouting threats of revenge.

Hitler, Ludendorff, Hess, and seven others went on trial for treason; Goering escaped to Sweden, to continue his drinking and drug taking. The trial began in February 1924, in a courtroom packed with reporters from the world's newspapers. What they saw was an insult to justice.

The judges and prosecutor were Nazi sympathizers. Instead of enforcing court rules, they allowed Hitler to turn the trial into a propaganda circus. He constantly interrupted and insulted government witnesses. He lectured the court whenever the spirit moved him, once for four hours nonstop. Unlike the others, who pleaded innocent, he took all "credit" for the putsch. The real criminals sat in offices in Berlin, he yelled. The Jews and the democratic republic were to blame for Germany's problems, not the patriotic Nazis.

The court's decision was a shocker. Despite the evidence, it acquitted Ludendorff of treason; the others were found guilty and freed on a suspended sentence. Hitler, the guiltiest of all, was given five years in Landsberg Prison.

Although Hitler was jailed, the trial backfired against the government. Until then, the Nazi movement had been confined to Bavaria. Now, with all the press coverage, Hitler's name became known in Germany and overseas. People who'd never heard of him suddenly made him their hero. A German spoke for thousands of his countrymen:

> In 1923 we heard the name of Adolf Hitler for the first time. . . . How that man Hitler spoke! Those days of his trial became the first days of my faith in Hitler. His behavior moved me to give him my whole faith. . . . Ever since those days I have fought and striven for my Fuehrer, Adolf Hitler. I shall readily give my all for him at any time he may demand it.

Landsberg Prison was like Landsberg Hotel for Hitler. As a political figure, he wasn't locked in a cell like a common criminal. He had a comfortable room without bars and could receive visitors during the day and see them in private. Each day's mail brought bouquets of flowers and baskets of food from well-wishers.

Prison was also a school for the future dictator. Hitler had been so busy during the past five years that he had little

Hitler, dressed in Bavarian folk costume, receives visitors in his cell in Landsberg Prison, 1924. Rudolf Hess, Hitler's personal secretary, is second from right.

time to collect his thoughts and plan for the future. Now he had plenty of leisure at government expense.

Hitler began to write a book to organize his thoughts and serve as a guide for fellow Nazis. For hours he'd pace the room, dictating to Rudolf Hess, who'd type out the notes each night. Since Hitler enjoyed talking, the book soon swelled to a thousand pages. At first he called it *Four and One-Half Years of Battle Against Lies, Stupidity, and Cowardice: Account Settled.* A publisher later shortened this mouthful to *Mein Kampf*, or *My Struggle.*

Mein Kampf is a nasty, mean-spirited book. It is dull and repetitious, and its earlier editions were filled with errors in grammar and spelling; one researcher counted over 164,000 errors. Although editors later corrected these errors, reading it is still a chore.

Yet *Mein Kampf* is one of the most important books of the twentieth century. In it, Hitler revealed his beliefs, methods, and plans. Racism, anti-Semitism, and the Big Lie are discussed there in all their ugliness. The author made no secret of what he'd do when he came to power: end democracy, abolish civil liberties, destroy the workers' trade unions, set up a police state. *Mein Kampf* preaches war and praises struggle as "the father of all things." God the Father, says Hitler, intended nations to fight until the stronger won. "He who wants to live must fight . . . and he who does not want to do battle in this world of eternal struggle does not deserve to be alive."

Hitler vowed in *Mein Kampf* to rebuild German military strength and take back every inch of land lost under the Treaty of Versailles. More, he promised to conquer a vast domain in Eastern Europe. Germany needed *Lebensraum,*

living space, for its growing population. The necessary land
and resources were available only in the Slavic countries,
especially in the Soviet Union. He scorned "the ridiculous
Slavs." He'd conquer them and settle Germans on their
lands. Those not needed as slaves would be killed.

Opponents ignored *Mein Kampf* as the ravings of a crack-
pot. They were wrong—dangerously, foolishly, wrong. For
the terrible thing is that Hitler was sincere. He meant what
he said, every word, and he would carry out his threats
when he came to power. No one should have been surprised, or claimed that he hadn't been given fair warning
of the savage world Hitler would create. Had *Mein Kampf*
been taken seriously, it might not have cost so many lives—
an estimated 125 lives for each word, 4,700 lives for each
page, one million lives for each chapter.

Hitler was pardoned and released from Landsberg in December 1924, after serving only nine months of his sentence. Times had changed during his stay in prison. He
returned to find his party banned and his lieutenants quar-
reling among themselves. Worse, the misery that had driven
people to his cause was easing. Foreign loans, especially
from the United States, had stabilized the mark, ending
inflation. Prices fell, trade increased, and food became plen-
tiful. For the first time since the war, the German people
were enjoying life. It was a gloomy Christmas for the Nazis.

Hitler wasn't discouraged. God, he felt, was testing his
worthiness to lead Germany. If anything, setbacks only convinced him of the rightness of his goal and made him work
harder.

Der Fuehrer lost no time in rebuilding and expanding the

party. His lieutenants were made to end their squabbles. Leaders who'd fled the country returned; Goering was more eager to help than ever. Schools were set up to train speakers, hundreds of "little Hitlers," who'd fan out across the country. The trainees memorized set speeches and rehearsed gestures in front of mirrors like actors. A network of clubs was started to attract members. Sports, stamp collecting, flying, gymnastics, sailing, hiking: the Nazis had a club for every interest. The SS was created as Hitler's personal bodyguard. In days to come, Heinrich Himmler, the young man who had once carried Hitler's standard into battle, would make the SS the most dreaded secret police force on earth.

In the meantime, Hitler had to persuade the government to lift its ban on the Nazi Party. He succeeded by promising not to shoot his way into power. There'd be no more putsches; instead, the Nazis would obey the law and compete in elections for the people's votes.

Only when it was too late did the government realize its mistake. Hitler promised to obey the law, not because he respected law, but in order to win support from German businessmen and the military. Yet his goal of establishing a dictatorship remained the same. Only the means and timing had changed. Ballots would replace bullets. He'd become chancellor through the ballot box, *then* make his revolution from within. Once in power, he'd use his office to destroy the Weimar Republic. In effect, democracy would sign its own death warrant and he'd be the executioner.

Nearly four years of work seemed wasted when national elections were held in 1928. After a hard campaign, the Nazis won only 12 of the Reichstag's 647 seats. At this rate, Hitler would grow old before coming to power. He prayed for another disaster to drive people into the Nazis' arms.

His prayers were answered when the United States econ-
omy took a nosedive. October 29, 1929, is known as Black
Tuesday in America. On that day prices tumbled on the
New York Stock Exchange, wiping out investors' holdings
overnight. Banks, unable to collect their business loans,
closed their doors; depositors lost everything, for bank ac-
counts weren't insured by the government in 1929. Factories
shut down, throwing their employees off the job. The country sank into the pit of the Great Depression.

Within a year, this disaster spread worldwide. Germany,
whose recovery had been fueled by American loans, was
devastated. Unemployment soared to over six million. Shanty
towns sprang up on the outskirts of cities, and people waited
for handouts on bread lines. One out of every two German
families suffered. To millions of decent, hardworking people, the Great Depression felt like the end of the world.

Germany had been on a roller coaster for fifteen years,
since 1914. War, defeat, revolution, putsches, and inflation
had come one after another. The Depression was the last
straw. Hatred blazed against a government that couldn't
provide work for people with families to support.

Desperate, confused people began to desert the republic
in ever-growing numbers. Many turned to the Communists,
who wanted to set up a Russian-style dictatorship. Millions
more flocked to Hitler. During the 1930 elections, his Nazis
captured 107 Reichstag seats. The democratic parties—
Democrats, Social Democrats, Catholic Center—lost heavily. The Weimar Republic was doomed.

The republic's enemies swung into action. Both the Nazis
and Communists sensed that their moment had come. A

great prize was suddenly within their reach. That prize was not Reichstag seats, but Germany and, in time, perhaps the world. Each party was determined to win at any cost.

A fierce struggle began for the minds and votes of the German people. The Nazis worked hardest, sparing no expense or effort in their propaganda war. Massive demonstrations, complete with huge bands and seas of blood-red flags, were held all over Germany. Countless handbills were passed out or tossed from speeding cars. Speakers kept up a steady barrage of words at rallies and on street corners. But Hitler took center stage. Wherever you turned, his eyes stared down from billboards of dazzling colors. Heavy black letters on a blood-red field made his message clear.

Der Fuehrer was a bundle of restless energy. He spoke for hours each day to crowds of tens of thousands. Using the slogan "Hitler Over Germany," he flew to rallies all over the country, the first politician to use the airplane in campaigning. Each rally always brought the same Big Lie. Jews, Communists, and democrats had ruined Germany! Trust Hitler to make things better! Don't think, only trust Hitler!

Millions did. Make no mistake about it: Hitler stirred real devotion. Theodore Abel, an American psychologist, collected hundreds of statements from early Nazis for his book, *Why Hitler Came to Power.* We read again and again of personal sacrifices for the benefit of the party. Men lucky enough to have jobs worked days to support their families, then gave the party eight or ten hours each night. One father, opposed to Hitler, beat his Nazi son unconscious. "Even if father kills me," the boy told his mother, "I shall remain true to Hitler."

Hitler also outclassed his opponents in the struggle for
the streets. During the years 1929–1932, party armies clashed
as never before. Nazi storm troopers and the Communist
Red Front turned Germany's towns and cities into battle-
grounds. They went far beyond the beer-hall brawls of the
1920s. Whenever they met now, the streets ran with blood.

The storm troopers' ranks swelled to over 400,000 by
1932. All types of men belonged: ex–Free Corps soldiers,
students, shopkeepers, the unemployed, professional criminals. Hitler put Ernst Roehm in charge and told him to
do what he knew best—fight.

Roehm's brown battalions marched every day, everywhere, singing and looking for trouble. Here is a stanza
from one song:

> The red brood, beat them to a pulp!
> Storm troopers are marching—clear the way!

Another song has this chilling verse:

> Sharpen the knives on the sidewalk,
> So that they can cut the enemy's bodies better.
> When the hour of revenge strikes,
> We shall be ready for mass murder.

Like their Fuehrer, these thugs meant what they said.
Opponents' meetings were broken up and their offices fire-
bombed. Even raids into "enemy territory" to tear down
posters and put up their own turned into full-scale battles.

Hitler wanted his men to act as terrorists. Violence wasn't
enough; they had to be cruel in order to paralyze the enemy
with fear and uncertainty. Storm troopers fought with anything that came into their hands: knives, brass knuckles,

Storm troopers holding the famous Blood Flag carried during the Munich Beer Hall Putsch. Storm troopers always carried two hats: a soft cap for everyday use, and a steel helmet for street fighting.

iron pipes, chains, belts, bottles of acid. Guns were used freely; a Nazi specialty was to have young women carry pistols into areas watched closely by the police. Once past the police, they'd give the pistols to storm troopers, who'd fire on the surprised enemy.

The police were nearly helpless in the face of such organized terrorism. Whenever Nazis were arrested, party newspapers hailed them as heroes and took up collections for their families. Bandaged and battered storm troopers were pictured as noble patriots. The dead—and hundreds died on each side—were given elaborate funerals and buried as martyrs.

Hitler's tactics paid off in the elections of July and November 1932. In the first election, the Nazis polled fourteen million votes, for 230 seats in the Reichstag. They lost two million votes, 34 seats, in the second election. Even so, Hitler still commanded the largest political party in Germany.

President Paul von Hindenburg decided that the Nazis could no longer be kept out of the government. On January 30, 1933, the old gentleman, who'd been Germany's supreme commander during the war, asked ex-Corporal Hitler to become chancellor. That night storm troopers held their mammoth victory parade down Berlin's Wilhelmstrasse.

As Hitler took their salute in the glare of torches, General Kurt von Schleicher, a former chancellor himself, sat gloomily at home. "This corporal will destroy Germany," he muttered. "It will have a horrible end." The general was a good prophet.

Although chancellor, Hitler still couldn't make his revolution from within. The Nazis held one third of the Reichstag's seats, far less than the two thirds needed to give him absolute power. In order to gain the additional seats, he needed two things. He needed new elections, which the ailing President Hindenburg, who called Hitler "the Bohemian corporal," scheduled for March 5, 1933. He also needed a crisis, something to stampede the voters into supporting a dictatorship. And if a crisis didn't come by itself, he'd manufacture one.

During the evening of February 27, just a week before the elections, the metal dome of the Reichstag building began to glow. Moments later, flames burst from every window and, catching the breeze, sent clouds of sparks into the black sky. All the firemen could do was watch the home of German democracy collapse into a heap of twisted metal and scorched brick.

We know today that the Reichstag fire was planned by Hitler and carried out on his orders. As soon as the election date was announced, he gave Heinrich Himmler an assignment. A team of his SS men was to sneak into the Reichstag through a heating tunnel and place gasoline bombs throughout the building. Destruction was to be total, removing any trace of arson.

Nazi propaganda blamed the Communists. Burning the Reichstag was said to be the signal for a putsch against the Hitler government. To prevent this, the Fuehrer enrolled fifty thousand storm troopers as special police to raid Communist offices throughout the country. Communist leaders were arrested and documents seized; forged papers were used as "evidence" to prove their guilt.

The Nazis did well in the elections that followed, winning over seventeen million votes, 288 Reichstag seats. Yet fifty-six percent of German voters still backed non-Nazi parties.

No matter. Hitler wasn't troubled by the people's lack of confidence. If they denied him an absolute majority at the polls, he'd take what he needed.

The Reichstag held its last meaningful session on March 23 in Berlin's Kroll Opera House. The purpose of this session, the Nazis explained, was to pass a single law, the Enabling Act. In effect, the Enabling Act called upon the Reichstag to commit suicide. Under its terms Hitler could suspend the constitution, change any law, and make new laws without consulting the people's representatives.

Der Fuehrer wasn't taking chances with the Enabling Act. The Communist members of the Reichstag were barred from the session. SS men checked members' credentials and stared at them hard, *very* hard. Storm troopers ringed the building, chanting "We want the bill, or fire and murder." The bill passed with the needed two-thirds majority— 441 in favor, 91 against.

Hitler now struck at whoever and whatever stood in his way. Germany's states were stripped of their powers and put under control of the central government in Berlin. Nazis took charge of all police forces. Trade union offices were occupied, the unions abolished, and union property seized.

Hitler next moved against Germany's political parties. The Communist Party was destroyed with a brutality unusual even for the storm troopers. Party members were forced to chew up and swallow dirty old socks. Many a man, with a pistol to his head, gagged down a quart of castor oil, which caused uncontrollable vomiting and occasionally death. By July 1933, all political parties except the Nazis were abolished. Anyone who tried to rebuild a political party, or start a new one, would feel the sting of Hitler's anger.

One hundred thousand people were arrested to begin with. Politicians, journalists, educators, factory workers—anyone who disagreed with Hitler—were swept up in the dragnet. Since there wasn't enough space in the jails, special camps were set up where prisoners could be concentrated—gathered—and easily guarded. These "concentration camps" soon became symbols of the Nazi terror. The first concentration camp was built at Dachau near Munich. By the end of 1933, similar camps were built close to every major German city.

Only President Hindenburg and the army high command stood between Hitler and total dictatorship. Both insisted that the storm troopers, now numbering three million, were getting out of hand. They were taking over businesses, looting, and beating up anyone they pleased. Ernst Roehm even spoke of the storm troopers' becoming the new German army. Professional soldiers were to be pushed aside in favor of his brown-shirted hoodlums, renamed the People's Army.

Hitler couldn't afford to antagonize the army. The storm troopers, with their light weapons and brawling ways, had conquered the streets of Germany for him, but there was no way they could conquer the world. Only the army leaders had the know-how to fight the wars he was planning.

Adolf Hitler used people as others use pencils and tubes of toothpaste. They weren't human beings to him, but *things*. When he had no further need of them, he threw them away or had them destroyed. The storm troopers had outlived their usefulness. To show the military his "good faith," he decided to murder their commanders, men who trusted him and had served him faithfully for years.

In the early hours of June 30, 1934, the Night of the

Long Knives began. SS squads rounded up storm trooper
leaders in Berlin and elsewhere. There were no charges, no
trials, no evidence. There were only firing squads. The
prisoners were lined up in fours, shot, and their bodies
carted away in butchers' tin-lined vans. Scores of men, not
knowing who'd condemned them, cried *"Heil Hitler!"* as
bullets tore into their bodies.

Hitler himself arrested the sleeping Roehm in a hotel
room near Munich. Roehm was shocked, unable to believe
that his friend had turned against him. Hadn't the Fuehrer
praised him? "I want to thank Heaven," he'd said, "for
having given me the right to call a man like you my friend
and comrade-in-arms."

But that was in the past. Roehm was taken to a prison
in Munich. There an SS man gave him a pistol with a
single bullet and said Hitler wanted him to shoot himself
within ten minutes. "If Adolf wants to kill me, let him do
the dirty work," Roehm snarled. Ten minutes later, the old
fighter fell before a hail of bullets. His last words were *"Mein
Fuehrer. Mein Fuehrer."*

One hundred fifty storm trooper leaders died during the
Night of the Long Knives. In addition, Hitler used the
opportunity to settle scores with about two thousand others.
Gustav von Kahr, who'd spoiled the 1923 putsch, was beaten
to death and his body dumped in a swamp near Dachau.
General von Schleicher, the former chancellor, and his wife
were gunned down in their living room. Then, in true
gangster style, the Reichstag arsonists were killed because
they knew too much. Hitler often buried his secrets with
the bodies of those who'd carried out his orders.

Der Fuehrer justified his actions a few days later in a

Hitler's legions, sworn to obey, wait for their Fuehrer's commands. Notice the SS insignia, two lighting bolts on a white field, on the helmet of the man at the lower right.

speech to the puppet Reichstag. The killings were necessary,
he explained, because the victims had been plotting against
him. The Reichstag members applauded, giving their blessing to another Big Lie.

President Hindenburg and the army chiefs were pleased.
When the president died at eighty-six, on August 2, 1934,
the military allowed Hitler to combine the offices of president and chancellor. As Hindenburg's successor, he also
became commander in chief of the *Wehrmacht*, Germany's
armed forces. The Nazi flag became Germany's official flag,
and every serviceman, from general to private, had to swear
an oath of obedience to Hitler:

> I swear by God this sacred oath to give my uncon-
> ditional obedience to Adolf Hitler, Fuehrer of the
> German Reich and nation, and supreme com-
> mander of the Wehrmacht, and I pledge my word
> as a brave soldier to lay down my life at any time
> for this oath.

No German fighting man had ever been made to take such
an oath. From then on, soldiers owed absolute obedience
not to the German nation, but to one man, and he of
doubtful sanity.

With that oath, the Third Reich was born. *Reich* means
empire. The First German Empire had existed during the
Middle Ages, coming to an end in 1806. The Second German Empire was created in 1871 and lasted to the end of
the First World War. The Third Reich, Hitler promised,
would be the greatest of all. It would last a thousand years.

LAND WITHOUT JUSTICE

HITLER DEVOTED THE FIRST YEARS OF HIS THOUSAND-YEAR Reich to setting up and perfecting a totalitarian system. *Totalitarianism* is a special form of dictatorship. An ordinary dictator is satisfied to control a government and rule without the people's consent; he rules basically by force. A totalitarian dictator wants more. He wants to control every aspect of people's lives, and, by so doing, shape them to his purposes as a potter shapes clay.

Der Fuehrer was determined to bring everything the German people thought and felt, believed and did, under his control. Any individual action or sign of creativity was seen as a crime, because it meant that there was still something outside his control. Such "crimes" were to be severely punished as warnings to others.

Hitler's Germany became a vast prison, although a prison where rewards were given for good behavior. But it was always understood that the German people had only one right, which was also a duty: to obey their leader's slightest whim. To obey always. To obey instantly. To obey without thought or question or complaint.

By the end of 1933, the freedoms that citizens of a democracy take for granted had vanished in Germany. The privacy of mail, telephone, and telegraph communications was violated by government eavesdroppers. Freedom of assembly and association was abolished. People could no longer gather or hold meetings without police approval. Every group, regardless of its purpose, was disbanded, and its members were forced to join a Nazi-dominated "league." Hundreds of these organizations sprang up, including the National Socialist Teachers', Veterans', Law Officers', Physicians', and Women's Leagues. Failure to belong to a Nazi group meant that you couldn't earn a living at a profession or enjoy a given pastime.

Hitler prevented Germans from traveling freely within their own country. Every adult had identification papers, complete with photo and fingerprints, that had to be carried always. To be without one's papers was a serious offense, punishable by arrest and jail. Every airport, train station, bus depot, and boat dock was watched by the police. Anyone using these facilities needed a good reason for traveling and had to show his papers at various points along the way. Whenever you stayed in a hotel, a policeman came around to see that your papers were in order.

Germans could no longer sell their labor or withhold it as they wished. Once Hitler smashed the trade unions, workers were forced to join the Nazi-controlled Labor Front. The Labor Front allowed no collective bargaining over wages, hours, and working conditions. Businessmen, in cooperation with the government, decided everything, and workers had to accept their decisions. Wages were lower than before the Great Depression, and workers were forced to give nearly half their earnings as dues to the Labor Front. Strikes were forbidden. Anyone who protested went to jail or, worse, to a concentration camp.

Yet most workers didn't think of themselves as unfree. They had vivid memories of the Depression, with all its hardships and humiliations. After years of joblessness, they were more interested in work, steady work at steady wages, than in civil rights.

Hitler gave them work and they were grateful; indeed, there were some who'd never voted for the Nazis but who confessed they loved him. He poured billions of marks into projects to cure unemployment. Towns echoed to the thump of jackhammers as old buildings were torn down and replaced by new homes, offices, theaters, and monuments. He built a vast network of *autobahns*—superhighways— that are still in use today. These roads not only joined the Reich's major cities, but would be vital communications links in wartime.

To prepare for that time, and to help the jobless, *der Fuehrer* began a massive military buildup. Government contracts made Germany's shipyards and aircraft plants come to life. Factories hummed, as tanks, artillery, and other weapons poured off the assembly lines. Coal mines and steel mills worked overtime, producing raw materials for the armaments industries. Hundreds of thousands of unemployed men in their twenties were drafted into the armed forces and taught to use the new weapons.

In return for good behavior, German workers enjoyed benefits once reserved for the wealthy. Hitler saw to it that a branch of the Labor Front called Strength Through Joy was created for the workers' recreation. Strength Through Joy provided cheaply, or at no charge, evening classes, dance performances, concerts, art exhibitions, and theater tickets. There was a wide range of sports activities, from gymnastics and parachuting to flying gliders, engineless aircraft that glide on the air currents. Men skilled in these sports later formed the backbone of the army's airborne divisions.

Strength Through Joy gave many workers the first vacations of their lives. In summer, cruise ships sailed to the Caribbean and South Atlantic; for example, a week's cruise to the beautiful island of Madeira off the coast of Morocco cost twenty-five dollars. Winter ski trips to the Bavarian Alps cost eleven dollars a week, complete with transportation, room, meals, ski rental, and skiing lessons.

These activities, though good in themselves, had a double purpose. They kept workers healthfully occupied and content, which increased factory production. They also allowed Hitler's snoopers to keep tabs on the workers at all times. A secret police spy was assigned to every activity to make sure everyone said the right things and thought the right thoughts.

Force and terror were always available to keep people in line if rewards failed. "Everyone," said Hitler, "must know that if he raises a hand to strike at the State, then certain death will be his lot."

The machinery of terror was controlled by Heinrich Himmler, Reich Leader SS. Born in 1900, this pale man with beady gray eyes and carefully trimmed mustache seemed like a mild-mannered schoolteacher. He never shouted or, apparently, laughed heartily. A serious man who couldn't stand the sight of blood, he loved animals. The thought of hunting made him sick to his stomach. It was cowardly and cruel, he insisted, to kill innocent, defenseless creatures. Even earthworms had a right to live. But not certain people. A fanatical racist, he believed that Jews and Slavs were lower than the lowliest animal and should be exterminated.

Himmler was a man after *der Fuehrer's* own heart—careful, hard-working, and obedient. Hitler saw in him the perfect police chief for a totalitarian state. When he appointed him head of the SS in 1929, his black-shirted bodyguard numbered only 280. Within a decade, Himmler turned the SS into a police force of a quarter million tough, disciplined men who'd do anything to keep the Fuehrer in power. Their motto was "Believe, Obey, Fight." This meant they'd carry out any order without thinking whether it was right or wrong.

Himmler wanted the SS to represent the best of the "Aryan race." Standards were high, and nine out of ten volunteers were rejected as unfit for the SS. Recruits had to be at least five feet six inches tall, meet certain standards of strength and endurance, and be free of physical or mental diseases. Above all, they must prove that both sides of their families had "pure Aryan blood" going back to the year 1750.

Before the Second World War, when entire SS divisions (the Weapons SS) fought alongside the army, the job of the SS was to detect, arrest, and punish anyone who might

Heinrich Himmler, Reich Leader SS, views Russian prisoners of war.

oppose Hitler. To do that, Himmler took charge of all Germany's police forces. The Order Police kept order— that is, dealt with traffic violations, crowd control, and safety-law enforcement. The Security Police, however, were the backbone of the Third Reich. It was they who kept the totalitarian system running, regardless of the people's wishes.

The Security Police were led by Himmler's assistant, General of Police Reinhard Tristan Eugen Heydrich. Born in 1904, Heydrich was a tall, handsome, blond man who combined high intelligence with devilish cruelty. Everything he did, good or evil, he did efficiently. Even fellow Nazis feared him. They called him "the Blond Beast" and "the Hangman." He earned both nicknames.

Heydrich's Security Police had several branches. Its criminal investigation sections tracked down murderers, arsonists, and thieves. Intelligence units spied on the Nazi Party itself and had "action squads" for special tasks such as the Reichstag fire and assassinations. Most feared was the *Gestapo*, or Secret State Police, who crushed opposition to Hitler's dictatorship.

Unlike the police forces of democratic countries, the SS was above the law. The Gestapo could commit any crime— as long as it served Hitler's plans. The Gestapo tried to sow suspicion, to build walls of distrust between people. It blanketed the country with thousands of agents and informers. Gestapo men impersonated Roman Catholic priests and heard confessions in church. An informer was stationed in every street and apartment house in every German town and city. He or she could be anyone: the janitor, the maid, a store clerk, or neighbor.

Informers snooped into everything. Did Herr Schmidt

hang out a swastika flag on *der Fuehrer's* birthday? How much, and how eagerly, did Frau Wolff contribute to the latest Nazi Party collection? Did old Herr Schneider forget to give the *Heil Hitler!* salute, which had replaced "Good day" as a greeting? Every shirking of a duty, every hint of disloyalty, was reported to the Gestapo for investigation.

Gestapo agents even listened to conversations in public places like railroad stations, restaurants, theaters, and street corners. Things became so bad that people developed "the German look," a quick over-the-shoulder glance to make sure no one was eavesdropping.

The Gestapo brought out the worst in people. Germans were encouraged to denounce one another for revenge or to gain some benefit. A man who wanted a coworker's job might come to the Gestapo with a made-up story—or a true one—that he'd spoken disrespectfully of *der Fuehrer*. One woman arranged to have agents listen outside an open window while her husband cursed the Nazis. He went to a concentration camp, and she won a divorce and all his property.

Someone wanted for questioning usually received a post-card ordering him to appear at Gestapo headquarters on a certain day and time. It was a summons you didn't ignore if you valued your life. In most cases you were questioned and released with a warning to watch your step, for the Gestapo knew everything about you. Even if you got off easily, you left headquarters with a dry mouth and shaking knees. You might also leave with a black eye and a swollen lip.

Minor offenses were often punished with public humil-iation. Buying in a Jewish-owned shop, for example, meant scrubbing a cobblestone street with a fingernail brush as crowds stood by, jeering. People wearing signboards listing their offenses were a common sight in German towns during the 1930s.

Serious offenses meant death. Telling anti-Nazi jokes carried the death penalty for the first offense. A man was hung for these twelve words:

> "Bernhard was arrested yesterday."
> "Bernhard! Such a *decent* fellow! Why?"
> "That's why."

Another man died for insulting the Fuehrer by saying: "What is the difference between Christianity and National Socialism? Simple. In Christianity one man [Christ] died for everybody. In National Socialism everybody dies for one man." Hitler had no sense of humor where his name or power was concerned.

The Gestapo showed no mercy to "enemies of the state." Everything it did was intended to terrify its victims and break down their resistance. Suspects' homes were raided in the middle of the night. Imagine how it must feel to be awakened at 3:30 A.M. by a ringing telephone. Now imagine shouting men breaking down the front door and dragging you from bed. As family and neighbors look on, you, still in bedclothes, are handcuffed, kicked out the door, and pushed into the back seat of a long black car with drawn windowshades.

Suspects were taken to secret prisons and cut off from contact with the outside world. It was like being swallowed by the earth. Try as they might, relatives were never told of a loved one's whereabouts or if they were still alive. No one told suspects their rights, for they had no rights. The idea of a suspect's speaking to a lawyer would have been laughable to the Gestapo.

Everything possible was done to make suspects confess their "crimes" and denounce others. Suspects were starved, deprived of sleep, spat upon. Trained torturers plunged the suspect into a living hell. Torturers used all the devices of the Middle Ages to break down their victims: thumb screws crushed fingers slowly, the boot crushed legs, the Iron Maiden punctured the body with hundreds of nails. People were stripped, doused with water, and given high-voltage electric shocks. Whippings went on for hours; often when one torturer tired, another took his place. One can see today dungeons where prisoners under torture gouged chunks of cement out of the walls with their bare hands.

Many died or went insane under this inhuman treatment. The lucky ones were released with a warning to keep quiet. Revealing where they'd been or what had happened to them meant death. In this way the Gestapo kept its secrets while keeping the German people in fear.

Each year the Gestapo sent thousands of people to concentration camps. Control of the camps had been taken from the storm troopers and given to the Death's Head SS, named for the skulls embroidered on their collars. Members of Death's Head units were specialists in brutality. Ordinary people flinch from the suffering of others, feeling that pain as their own. Not concentration camp guards. They were taught to inflict suffering coldly, efficiently, without any show of human feeling. They had an evil reputation in Germany. Even small children dreaded the Death's Head SS. A nursery jingle ran: "Dear Lord, make me religious so that I won't go to Dachau."

People were sent to Dachau and some fifty other camps without trial and for as long as Hitler wanted to keep them there. In addition to Dachau, the largest camps were: Sachsenhausen, near Berlin; Buchenwald, near Weimar; and Mauthausen, built near Linz after Hitler took over Austria in 1938. An evil in themselves, concentration camps should not be confused with the death camps built after 1942 for the systematic extermination of Europe's Jewish people.

Concentration camps *looked* evil even from a distance. Built amid open fields, each was surrounded by high fences of electrified barbed wire. Watchtowers with powerful searchlights and machine guns overlooked the camp and its outside approaches. At night, searchlight beams crisscrossed the whole area. Guards patrolled with flashlights and savage German shepherd and Doberman pinscher dogs. People caught trying to escape were thrown onto the electrified fences, given to the dogs, or kept for "special treatment"— slow death by torture or in the starvation cells.

Prisoners wore rags or, if lucky, black-and-white-striped uniforms. They lived in long, unpainted sheds of rough pine boards. The sheds were unheated, drafty, and leaked when it rained. Prisoners slept not in beds, but on straw-filled sacks set on wooden shelves arranged in three levels, one above the other. A shelf held five people, each in an area less than a yard wide. They lay on their sides, without blankets, cramped and unable to move. When they woke up, everyone's hands and legs were numb and their backs ached. Barracks and sleeping shelves swarmed with roaches, lice, and rats. People were always scratching or trying to doctor rat bites without medicine. There were no washing facilities. A toilet was just a wooden plank with a hole set

Dachau barracks. Thousands of men like these slept crammed onto wooden shelves in this concentration camp outside the German city of Weimar.

over a pit that served hundreds of prisoners. There was always a lineup and the odor was sickening.

Although the Death's Head SS ate well, their prisoners were kept on the verge of starvation. Breakfast and lunch in most cases were weak black coffee with a crust of bread; often the bread had holes in it gnawed by rats. Dinner was coffee, turnips, and potato peelings seasoned occasionally with rotten salt fish. The fortunate prisoners worked at collecting garbage from the SS mess halls and had the privilege of eating scraps from the garbage pails. An ex-Dachau prisoner has written: "In the camps, everything human disappeared. We were merely objects. No normal mortal can imagine how we were treated."

The brutality and suffering never stopped. At daybreak, SS guards with leather whips drove the prisoners out of their barracks for roll call. People in flimsy clothes stood at attention in all weathers until officers were satisfied that everyone was present, which might take hours. On command, prisoners had to sing dirty songs about themselves, do exercises until they fainted, and watch punishments.

There was plenty to see. Breaking the smallest rule, or none at all, brought savage punishment. As fellow prisoners watched, not daring to move a muscle, people were clubbed, whipped, or, in winter, made to stand naked in snow overnight. To set an example, others were sentenced to solitary confinement. They were locked in tiny cement cells in which they could neither stand up straight nor lie down. There they stooped, naked, bent over for days at a time in darkness, unable to relax or sleep. Executions for stealing a scrap of food took place every week; bodies were kept hanging on the gallows until they became skeletons. Prisoners were always being "shot while trying to escape."

Hitler made sure that every part of Germany had its little corner of hell. There was even a concentration camp—Ravensbrueck—reserved for women. Although the camp commanders were men, the guards were mostly SS women. Big, strong, and well-fed, these women were as brutal as any of the Death's Head SS. Yet they were gentle compared to Dorothea Binz, the commander's assistant. A former prisoner described her:

> Whenever she appeared somewhere, one literally felt the touch of evil. She would move slowly among the ranks, her [whip] behind her back, searching with menacing little eyes for the weakest and most frightened woman simply to beat her black and blue.

At first Ravensbrueck held only German women. But once the Second World War began, prisoners came from everywhere in Nazi-occupied Europe. Among these were Geneviève de Gaulle, niece of French General Charles de Gaulle, and Gemma La Guardia Gluck, sister of New York City's Mayor Fiorello La Guardia. Heinrich Himmler's own sister, Olga, was sent to Ravensbrueck for falling in love with a Polish army officer.

Animals were better treated in the Third Reich than "enemies of the State." Hitler, like Himmler, loved animals and made laws for their protection; for example, restaurants must kill lobsters and crabs quickly in boiling water to avoid needless suffering.

No laws protected concentration camp inmates. For them, as for millions of others accused of disloyalty, Germany's justice system had been corrupted. Hans Frank, Minister of Justice, was right when he said, "Our constitution is the will of the Fuehrer."

Those not taken straight to a concentration camp found that the courts served Hitler, not justice. Instead of being treated as innocent until proven guilty, as in democratic countries, the accused had to prove their innocence. That was impossible, since everything had been settled before the trial began. No one was on the side of the accused. Defense lawyers belonged to the National Socialist Law Officers' League and had taken a loyalty oath to Hitler. Judges, all Nazis with swastikas on their robes, shouted at the accused and insulted them.

There was nobody to appeal to if you were wronged by the government, police, SS, or courts. Hitler had turned Germany into a land without justice.

A century before Hitler, the French dictator Napoleon said that one could do anything with bayonets except sit on them. He, like Hitler, understood that a dictator, to succeed, must not only enslave his people's bodies, he must also enslave their minds. He must brainwash them, wiping away old beliefs and replacing them with his own ideas. They must want to do his will; indeed, they must *love* obeying him.

Hitler gave the job of brainwashing the German people to one of his most trusted henchmen: Dr. Paul Joseph Goebbels. Hitler had recognized Goebbels' talents when they met in 1925, and made him his propaganda advisor. An educated man, Goebbels had attended six universities and earned a Doctor of Philosophy degree in literature. Small, dark-skinned, with a thin face, large nose, and crippled left leg, he was nicknamed "the Poison Dwarf," "the Mouse-Doctor,"

*Dr. Paul Joseph Goebbels, Nazi Minister of Propa-
ganda, during one of his speeches. The "Poison
Dwarf" was almost as good at rousing a crowd as
Hitler himself.*

and "Hitler's Mickey Mouse." Like his Fuehrer, Goebbels dreamed of becoming an artist, only one who used words instead of paints. He wrote several novels and plays, all failures. Failure made him bitter, and bitterness turned him into a hater. He grew to despise humanity, filling his diary with remarks like "Life is dirt" and "The world is disgusting." When Hitler came to power, Goebbels became Minister of Propaganda.

The Mouse-Doctor knew what he had to do. To shape the people's thoughts, he had to get control of the information they received. Soon every means of spreading ideas and information was taken over by the Ministry of Propaganda. Now it decided what was true or false. And anyone who disagreed would have to explain to the Gestapo.

Goebbels struck first at freedom of the press. In May 1933 he staged an event that shocked civilized people everywhere. On May 10, a Wednesday, members of Nazi youth organizations invaded public and school libraries to weed out "un-German" books. Anything by a Jewish or Communist author was un-German in their eyes. Anything that praised peace and condemned war, or spoke well of freedom and democracy, or saw good in other nations, had no place in the Third Reich.

Books were carried in torchlight parades to blazing funeral pyres of crisscrossed logs. Then, as the authors' names were read out, their works were thrown into the fires while bystanders cheered and bands played Nazi tunes.

Every city had its book burning. In Berlin, where the Mouse-Doctor took charge personally, works by some of Germany's finest authors were destroyed. Among these were books by Dr. Sigmund Freud, father of psychiatry, the sci-

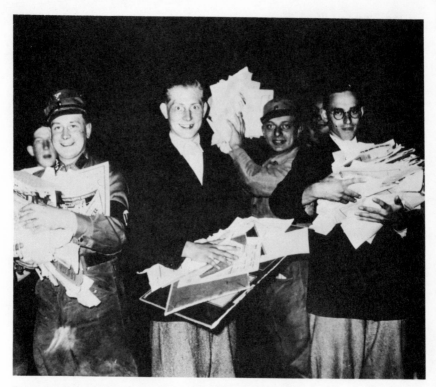

Storm troopers and Hitler Youth burn "un-German" books in 1933.

ence that treats diseases of the human mind. Erich Maria Remarque's *All Quiet on the Western Front,* a gripping account of trench fighting, went into the flames because it told of the horrors of the First World War. Also burned were American writings, including those by Helen Keller, a deaf-blind author of antiwar books, and Jack London, a champion of free labor unions.

Goebbels quickly abolished freedom of the press in Germany. All books, magazines, and newspapers had to follow the Nazi line or face destruction. Goebbels tuned the press like a musical instrument. At the start of each week, he decided what news the German people would receive and how it would be presented. Nazi successes were exaggerated. Nazi failures were omitted or explained away with lies.

The Mouse-Doctor had the press spread slogans as part of the Big Lie. Slogans are catch phrases that are easily remembered. Repeated often enough, they become automatic, making it unnecessary to think about whether they are true or false or just silly. Goebbels hammered away with old Nazi slogans and invented new ones as needed. A half century later, there are elderly Germans who still remember them vividly. Some of the more famous slogans were:

"Ein Reich, ein Volk, ein Fuehrer" ("One nation, one people, one leader").

"Fuehrer, command us! We will follow!"

"The Jews are our misfortune."

"Juda verrecke!" ("Slaughter the Jews!")

One book was favored above all in the Third Reich. *Mein Kampf* became a bestseller as soon as Hitler came to power. You saw it everywhere in cheap paperback editions and bound in leather with gold lettering on the cover. Children on birthdays, elderly couples on anniversaries received it as gifts. A Fuehrer decree ordered every couple to buy a copy when they took out a marriage license. Millions of copies were sold each year, although seldom were read from cover to cover. Yet it was something you had to own to show that you were a good German, and to keep the Gestapo from your door.

Sales of *Mein Kampf* made Hitler a millionaire. He also became rich from postage stamps. Most German postage stamps bore his picture. For each of the billions of stamps sold each year, he received a couple of pennies for allowing his picture to be used.

Goebbels made sure that the Fuehrer's voice followed people everywhere. Millions of inexpensive radios were produced, which people were expected to buy for their homes. Loudspeakers were set up in factories and on city streets. Whenever the Fuehrer spoke, traffic came to a standstill and people stopped what they were doing. Not listening to Hitler, or listening to forbidden broadcasts, made you a "radio criminal." Anyone caught tuning in to a foreign station went to prison. Usually they were reported by Nazi Party "radio wardens," whose duty was to snoop on the listening habits of neighbors.

The arts, too, were made to serve totalitarianism. Hitler, the failed painter, thought himself the greatest art expert of all time. As such, he decided how artists could express themselves and what the German people could enjoy.

Goebbels set up the Reich Culture Chamber to carry out his master's wishes in the arts. Those denied membership or expelled from the Chamber were forbidden to pursue an artistic career. They couldn't write books, recite poetry, direct films, compose music, act in plays, paint pictures, or carve statues. The Gestapo had a special branch that policed the arts. Those forbidden to create were watched by undercover agents. The least sign of disobedience brought a one-way ticket to Dachau. Some artists, desperate at having to give up their work, committed suicide.

Hitler's ideas of beauty were forced upon the German people. Blacklists were drawn up by the Propaganda Ministry of "degenerate art"—anything that offended the Fuehrer or failed to show the superiority of the Aryan race. What followed was a massacre of artworks.

Over 16,000 paintings disappeared from museum walls, of which 6,500 were burned or kicked to pieces. Among them were works by the giants of modern art, people like Pablo Picasso, Vincent van Gogh, Paul Klee, and Joan Miró. Their places were taken by works of Nazi artists showing marching storm troopers, scenes from Nazi history, and the Fuehrer in countless poses. One picture was reproduced by the millions. It showed Hitler on horseback as a knight in shining armor, fearless and strong, going out to conquer the world.

These were also favorite themes in films, along with the glorification of war and anti-Semitism. Films like *The Eternal Jew* showed Jews as beasts worthy of extermination. In music, jazz was forbidden as "savage Negro noise"; orchestras had to give up the saxophone, an instrument of "Negroid savagery." Orchestras could play only the German classics. The operas of Richard Wagner, Hitler's favorites, were performed often and well during the Third Reich. Dances like the Black Bottom and Charleston were forbidden as creations of inferior people from the jungles of Africa.

Goebbels' most important task was to glorify the Fuehrer. Every day in every way Germans were brainwashed into believing that Hitler was the greatest person who'd ever lived. The Propaganda Ministry praised him to the heavens. He was all-good, all-wise, all-knowing, and all-powerful, like God. "He alone is never mistaken," said Goebbels. "He is always right. . . . He is above us all. He is always like a star above us."

Not to be outdone, other Nazi leaders praised Hitler at every opportunity. Rudolf Hess bawled, "Adolf Hitler is Germany and Germany is Adolf Hitler. And Germany is our God on earth." Hans Frank used some Nazi logic: "Hitler is lonely. So is God. Hitler is like God." Youth leader Baldur von Schirach added, "Your name, my Fuehrer, is the happiness of youth. Your name, my Fuehrer, is for us everlasting life."

The propaganda worked—so much so that many Germans worshipped Hitler. People lit candles and prayed to him in the "Hitler corners" of their homes. Sunny, cloudless days were known as "Hitler weather." Pregnant women called his name to relieve their labor pains. Newspapers reported about a talking dog who knew that it had a friend. When asked "Who is Adolf Hitler?" it replied "My Fuehrer," for he had made laws against cruelty to animals.

Had people known about the real Hitler, they might have thought differently. Their heroic Fuehrer was afraid of being alone in the dark. Before going to sleep, he'd have SS men search the bedroom to make sure "he" wasn't there; Hitler never said who "he" was. Sometimes the tyrant would wake up screaming, "He! He! He's been here!" His lips would turn blue, and sweat would stream down his face. He'd babble strange words, then sit still, only his lips working, until his panic left.

The Germans' all-good Fuehrer was fascinated with blood and death. He'd have his favorite physician, Dr. Theodor Morell, draw his blood and save it in test tubes, which he'd stare at for hours. When criminals were executed, he watched films of their death agonies in his private movie theater; the slower they died, the better he enjoyed the films. He often spoke of severed heads, and was responsible for bringing back the headsman's ax as a means of execution.

Germany's all-wise Fuehrer had childlike ways and tastes. Addicted to sweets, he ate huge amounts of candy and syrup-filled chocolate bonbons; he always put at least seven tea-spoons full of sugar into each cup of tea. For relaxation, he watched movies and played with toys. His favorite movies were *King Kong* and Walt Disney's *Snow White and the Seven Dwarfs*. Guests at the Chancellery might find him lying on the floor surrounded by blocks. The master of the Third Reich formed these into buildings, which he'd then destroy with a miniature cannon. He also used the cannon to mow down armies of toy "enemy" soldiers.

The all-powerful Fuehrer hadn't learned much about self-control since his teenage years with Kubizek in Linz. He had a hair-trigger temper, and anything could set off a temper tantrum in which he seemed to be losing his mind. If someone disagreed with him about the name of a tune, or if he found a speck of dirt in his office, his face would turn beet-red. He'd scream at the top of his voice, kick over furniture, and foam at the mouth. Often he'd drop to the floor, thrashing his feet and pounding his fists on the carpet.

This side of his character, of course, was a closely guarded
secret known only to his inner circle.

Hitler's power touched the German people in the most
private details of their lives. In totalitarian Germany nothing, really, was private. Whom should you marry? Should
you be *allowed* to marry? How many children may you
have? How will your children be raised? The answers to
these questions, and to scores of others like them, became
the business of the Nazi state.

Hitler believed that women were inferior to men. While
still a teenager, he'd argued that women could not think
logically, because they were ruled by their emotions. Education was wasted on them, and giving them responsibility
was like trusting a rabbit to fly an airplane. The perfect
woman, in the Fuehrer's eyes, was "a cute, cuddly, naïve
little thing—tender, sweet, and stupid."

She must also be a mother. Hitler insisted that women's
role was to become breeding machines for his Thousand-
Year Reich. Children were necessary to the Reich's future
as warriors and as parents of warriors. Thus childlessness,
whether in married or single women, became unpatriotic,
a weakening of the nation.

Hitler encouraged early marriages and large families. He
saw to it that young "Aryan" couples received government
loans to set up housekeeping. With each child born, one
quarter of the loan became a gift; cash bonuses were paid
for every child over the fourth.

The SS had no choice about marriage. Himmler ordered
his men to marry early and father as many children as
possible. Their brides-to-be had to pass strict medical in-

spections to guarantee their ability to bear children. Like the men, they had to prove "racial purity" to the year 1750.

Himmler reviewed all SS marriage applications, signing the licenses personally. He also set up the Spring of Life, "baby farms" where women became mothers without marrying their SS lovers, who might also have wives of their own. There was no shame in having children out of wedlock. Unwed mothers were rewarded for their services to the state, and their children were cared for by the government.

Married mothers were special people in the Third Reich. Women with four or more children received a medal, the Motherhood Cross, which entitled them to special treatment wherever they went. Passengers on crowded trains and buses had to give them their seats. They might go to hospitals for free medical treatment and, later, live in special sections of old-age homes. The slogan "I have donated a child to the Fuehrer" commanded instant attention and respect.

Respect, however, belonged only to healthy people with healthy families; all others were branded "poisoners of the nation's blood." The handicapped had no rights in Nazi Germany. Men and women suffering from birth defects, retardation, blindness, and incurable physical and mental illnesses were not allowed to have children. They were *sterilized*, made to undergo an operation to prevent them from becoming parents. Thousands were sterilized each year against their will.

Hitler had no sympathy for the helpless. War was coming, and every resource would be needed for the struggle. Anyone unable to aid the war effort didn't deserve to live, he said. They were "useless mouths" who ate precious food and occupied hospital beds needed for wounded soldiers. Such people were given *euthanasia*.

Euthanasia is Greek for "good death"; we'd call it "mercy killing." Hospitals, mental institutions, and old-age homes were ordered to prepare lists of "useless" patients: the incurably ill, crippled, insane, retarded, senile. These people were then taken away in buses and ambulances and handed over to the SS. In batches of fifty, they were walked, carried, and wheeled into small, windowless rooms and killed with poison gas. Between seventy and one hundred thousand harmless, helpless Germans were gassed from 1939 to 1945. The exact number is unknown, because the killings were kept secret. All the victims' families received was a death certificate and an urn of ashes.

Hitler never had children. For several years the only woman in his life was his niece, Geli. Geli, an attractive blond in her early twenties, was the daughter of Angela Raubal, his half-sister. Geli and "Uncle Ali," as she called him, lived together until she shot herself in 1931 for an unknown reason. Her death nearly drove Hitler to suicide. As a result he became a vegetarian, unable to look at meat without becoming ill. Meat stew he called "corpse soup"; suckling pig reminded him of "roast baby."

Hitler began to live with twenty-year-old Eva Braun in 1932. Eva, who'd been a clerk in a photographer's shop, was a handsome, soft-spoken woman. She was the only person who could get him to relax. He cared for her, bossed her, pampered her. But he never allowed himself to be seen with her in public, for that might have caused a scandal. Eva became his wife a day before they committed suicide in April 1945.

Parents gave life to children, but in fact those lives belonged to *der Fuehrer.* Hitler wanted to control Germany's children in every way possible. Not that they mattered in themselves. No, they could live or die, for all he cared. What mattered was that by starting early enough he could raise them to be a "Master Race" of world conquerors.

Education was the key to the future. Hitler the school dropout despised learning, believing it spoiled the young and made them soft. Literature and poetry, the sciences and languages, were useless for his purposes. His ideas about education were simple—and savage:

> My teaching is hard. Weakness must be cut away. . . . I want a violent, arrogant, fearless, cruel youth, who must be able to suffer pain. Nothing weak or tender must be left in them. Their eyes must show once again the free, magnificent beast of prey. . . . They shall learn to overcome the fear of death through the most severe tests.

Germany's education system, once among the world's finest, was taken over by the Nazis and ruined. Jewish teachers lost their jobs instantly, while the others were made to join the National Socialist Teachers' League. Their schoolrooms became extensions of the local storm trooper headquarters. Swastika flags hung in the front of every room. Portraits of *der Fuehrer* glared from the walls. All classes began and closed with the stiff-armed *Heil Hitler!* salute.

Parents went along with the new system, or else. Hitler declared that parents who didn't want their children brought up as little Nazis were "unfit." Their children were taken away and placed in foster homes or orphanages.

Teachers who disagreed were publicly humiliated and

dragged off to concentration camps. Storm troopers took a young teacher from his classroom in one town. He was made to stand at attention outside the school. Then, with everyone watching, the bullies paraded by, each one spitting in his face. When his mother was asked what crime he'd committed, she sobbed, "Nothing! Nothing at all! He refused to become a Nazi. He couldn't bring himself to go along with them. That was his crime." Most teachers, however, fearing for their jobs and their lives, did go along.

Mein Kampf became required reading in all grades. Classes read it, discussed it, wrote compositions about it, and, after the last chapter, started over on page one.

Textbooks were rewritten and every subject taught from a Nazi point of view. Racism and anti-Semitism were drummed into youngsters' heads. They learned that they, as Aryans, belonged to the Master Race destined to rule the world. Jews were to be feared and hated. For example, children in lower grades read a colorful picture book, *Trust No Fox and No Jew*. Another popular book was *The Poisonous Mushroom*, showing Jews as ugly "race-poisoners."

Hitler's children learned that war is good and necessary. Even harmless-seeming subjects were given a warlike twist. Nature study stressed not beauty and cooperation, but brutality and competition. Schoolchildren read a poem describing life as a struggle between weak and strong:

> *"Please," begged the victim, "let me go,*
> *For I am such a little foe."*
> *"No," said the victor, "not at all.*
> *For I am big and you are small."*

The poem's lesson is that bullies are best. It teaches that the strong have the right to destroy the weak. Spiders catch flies and eat them without mercy. Sparrows in turn catch spiders, and so on throughout nature, until the mighty Aryans conquer weaker races. The Nazis taught that love, tenderness, and compassion were evil.

Hitler worship was the duty of children as well as adults. Youngsters had to say *"Heil Hitler!"* at least fifty times a day, as if calling upon the Lord. Kindergarten classes praised *der Fuehrer* each day with grace:

> *Fuehrer, my Fuehrer, bequeathed to me by God,*
> *Protect and preserve me as long as I live!*
> *You have rescued Germany from deep despair.*
> *I thank you for my daily bread.*
> *Abide long with me. Forsake me not.*
> *Fuehrer, my Fuehrer, my faith and my light,*
> *Heil, my Fuehrer!*

Elementary pupils celebrated his birthdays in song:

> *Adolf Hitler is our savior, our hero.*
> *He is the noblest being in the whole world.*
> *Our Hitler is our Lord,*
> *Who rules a brave new world.*

Each German home had its live-in Gestapo informer. Children learned in school that the Fuehrer came first, above even love for their parents. Boys and girls were expected to report their parents for failure to give the Hitler salute and other acts that might signal disloyalty. Parents went to jail, or to Dachau, on the word of their own children.

One father's life was innocently ruined. A schoolboy in Berlin in 1934 interrupted a hate lesson on Jews. "My daddy," he said, "says Jews are not damnably vile." By dismissal time, Daddy was in Gestapo custody.

Hitler filled the young persons' after-school hours. Within days of taking power, all youth groups were abolished and replaced by the Hitler Youth for boys and the League of German Maidens for girls. Everyone of school age had to belong to a Nazi youth organization or be placed in an orphanage.

The Hitler Youth had three branches. Younger boys belonged to the Little Ones (ages six to ten) or to the Young Folks (ages ten to fourteen). These were nothing like our Boy Scouts, although some of their activities were the same. Hitler's children went through a difficult course of physical training to toughen their bodies. The course included running, swimming, soccer, marching in military formation, and long-distance hiking; thirteen-year-olds had to march a minimum of ten miles a day. As they marched, they chanted, "We are nothing! Our nation is everything!" Their minds were toughened with more of the racism they'd learned in school.

A youth group's "report card" was more important than any from school. Each boy carried a Book of Deeds listing his every accomplishment and failure, however small. A poor mark made you a bad person, a traitor to yourself, your group, and your Fuehrer. Good marks were rewarded with a man-sized dagger with the swastika insignia on the handle and the slogan "Everything for Germany" etched into the blade.

Senior boys (ages fourteen to eighteen) belonged to the

*"HEIL HITLER!" A detachment of Hitler Youth
gives the Nazi salute during a rally in the mid-1930s.*

Hitler Youth itself. Gone now were the days of childhood. *Der Fuehrer* wanted his teenagers to be the meanest, harshest on earth. All human feelings for non-Germans were to be driven from them. He commanded his youth to be swift as greyhounds, tough as leather, and hard as steel. They must be Aryan "Supermen."

The program of the Hitler Youth was simply military basic training scaled down for teenagers. The Hitler Youth had many sections, each a copy of a military unit. As in the army, it trained cavalry, scouting, signals, ski, mountaineering, sniping, and motorcycle units. Naval cadets learned about ships' engines, sailing, and navigation. Boys prepared for the Luftwaffe by learning parachuting and piloting small planes and gliders.

The Hitler Youth became familiar with weapons. Rifles, pistols, and light machine guns were to them what baseball bats and hockey sticks are to boys in other lands. Hours were spent on the target range, shooting from a standing position or prone on the ground, as in combat. Other important skills were throwing dummy hand grenades and the martial arts: boxing, wrestling, judo.

Everyone marched. In all weather and seasons, squads of Hitler Youth tramped Germany's roads behind their swastika flags. A sixteen-year-old marched at least fifteen miles a day with a ten-pound pack, singing, "God is struggle and struggle is our blood, and that is why we were born."

Training for the battlefield was realistic. Gregor Ziemer, an American educator, once visited the Hitler Youth during combat exercises directed by storm trooper veterans of the First World War. It was an eye-opener. Ziemer saw a "prisoner" brought to headquarters. He was gagged and his eyes were taped shut. As he walked, boys jeered and kicked him along with muddy boots. The storm trooper leader grinned, explaining that they were preparing for war, not enjoying a tea party. "I don't expect the other side to grant my boys mercy when they get captured," he said. "The idea is not to get caught." Beatings gave his boys a healthy fear of getting caught.

Unfortunately, some boys were caught—caught dead. At one campsite, a ten-year-old who'd forgotten the password was shot by a sentry. When questioned by the police, the fourteen-year-old killer said he'd used his pistol against a "spy" sneaking into the camp. He was only doing his duty, like a true Hitler soldier. The police agreed and refused to charge him with a crime.

The Hitler Youth were educated for victory or death. In countless ways they learned that a German man must be as eager to die as to kill for his Fuehrer. Their oaths, songs, and poems spoke of glorious death in battle. He who held back, who loved life better than glory, wasn't a true man.

These weren't just words to be spoken and then forgotten. We know of boys who preferred to die rather than let down their Fuehrer. Once a boy ill with pneumonia was forced to go on a long march in the rain. He collapsed and, near death, refused help from the family doctor. He lay in bed, burning with fever and shouting *"Heil Hitler!"* Again and again he'd cry, "Let me die for Hitler. I must die for Hitler!" He'd lost the will to live and soon had his wish.

The boy's sisters were prepared for motherhood and war in the League of German Maidens. To become healthy mothers of healthy warriors, girls had a full program of athletics: diving, swimming, hiking, throwing the javelin.

Girls' camps were located near those of the Hitler Youth. Each fall, with the end of the summer camping season, the number of unwed mothers-to-be rose dramatically. A civil defense program prepared girls for war with lessons in first aid and air-raid precautions, such as putting out fire bombs with sand.

It was made clear, however, that females were second-class citizens in the Third Reich. Married women doctors and government officials were fired when Hitler came to power. Women could not be judges or members of juries, because, said a Fuehrer order, "they cannot think logically." Nearly all women were denied a chance to attend a university. Women's only purpose was to breed soldiers for *der Fuehrer*.

People left the youth movement when they turned nineteen. All nineteen-year-olds owed the state a year of unpaid work. Hitler Youth graduates helped with the harvests and improved the land, draining swamps and replanting forests. This Service Year was followed by two years in the army. Women worked as housekeepers, nursemaids, and farm helpers.

Thus Hitler took charge of Germany's young people during their formative years. Having shaped their minds and trained their bodies, he believed he'd own them unto death.

In millions of cases, he was right.

THE MARCH OF
CONQUEST

SOMETIME IN THE LATE 1920S, ADOLF HITLER SHARED HIS
private thoughts with his closest aides. They sat in his Munich apartment, remembering the past and dreaming of the
future. The Fuehrer, growing serious, began to talk of
war.

Certainly he wanted war—and what a war it would be!
He'd begin by scrapping the Treaty of Versailles and taking
back Germany's lost territories. But he wouldn't stop there.
He *couldn't* stop, because the need for battle was part of
him, like his flesh and bones. "We shall attack, and it
doesn't matter whether we go ten or a thousand kilometers
beyond the present borders. For whatever we gain, it will
always be the starting point for new battles."

Each gain the starting point for new battles! Here was the

true Hitler. He'd never be satisfied until he ruled the world, and perhaps not even then.

As Germany's ruler, Hitler set out to make his dreams reality. His first victories came cheaply, bloodlessly. They were the result, not of fighting, but of bluffing and threats. Out of these early successes grew the Second World War, costing the lives of at least thirty-five million Europeans.

Yet this tragedy needn't have happened, for Hitler could have been stopped anytime before 1939. Although rearmament was going ahead full blast, Germany was still not ready for a full-scale war. Had the Allies of the First World War, joined by the United States, acted in time, they could have ended the Hitler threat forever.

But action meant a willingness to fight, and the Allies' willingness to fight was practically gone. Leaders and peoples remembered the horrors of the last war. Reminders of that tragedy were all around, in the vast cemeteries and in the broken bodies of millions of disabled veterans. The land, too, was wounded. Thousands of square miles of France and Belgium lay devastated years after the Armistice. Trenches remained like badly healed scars, long gashes in the earth covered with green grass and spotted with crimson poppies. Even today each spring planting brings up its harvest of rusty helmets, unexploded shells, and human bones. Sensible people who'd suffered so terribly vowed, "Never again!"

Hitler understood their fear and how to use it against them. He'd bully, and threaten, and take over small countries, gambling that the democracies would pay almost any price to avoid another war. In time, of course, they'd have to fight as the danger drew near. But by then Germany's war machine would be unbeatable. Although mentally disturbed, *der Fuehrer* was a keen politician who knew how to take advantage of others' weaknesses.

Hitler began his march of conquest timidly, like a skater testing thin ice. The Versailles Treaty had forbidden Germany to station troops in the Rhineland, an industrial area along the border with France. This arrangement weakened Germany's defenses and, treaty or not, it had to be changed.

On March 7, 1936, Hitler sent his troops into the Rhineland. It was a dangerous move, for the French army, still the strongest in Europe, could easily have wiped out the Nazis. *Der Fuehrer* knew that had the French marched, "we would have had to withdraw with our tails between our legs." In fact, he'd ordered his generals to retreat at the first sign of opposition. None came.

The French spoke harshly but did nothing. And since Hitler feared only their guns, he knew that his gamble had paid off.

Such an easy victory made the tyrant bolder. Early in 1938, he looked toward his homeland. Austria was not the same country he'd left as a young man. At the end of the First World War, the Allies had broken up the Austro-Hungarian Empire. Hungary became independent. Large chunks of imperial territory went to the newly created countries of Czechoslovakia, Poland, and Yugoslavia. All that remained was Austria itself, a small, weak nation.

Hitler decided to make Austria a territory of the Third Reich. The majority of Austrians spoke German, which made them Germans in his eyes. Besides, he needed Austrian manpower and industry for future conquests.

In February 1938, Hitler met Austrian Chancellor Dr.

Kurt von Schuschnigg to discuss relations between their two countries. His face flushed, he worked himself into a frenzy the moment he set eyes on the dignified statesman. The Austrian government must, *must* stop opposing *Anschluss*, union with Germany, he shouted. If it didn't go along with his plans, he'd attack immediately. It was no use looking to the democracies for aid. France and England would sell out anyone to avoid war, he said.

Schuschnigg, feeling that he had no choice, gave in to Hitler's demands. On March 11, 1938, he turned the government over to Austrian Nazis. The next day the German army crossed the border.

Hitler's return to Vienna was one of the high points of his life. Here was revenge, and how sweet it tasted! His black limousine glided along streets covered with flowers, streets he'd roamed as a tramp. No one in Vienna could ignore him now. No one *dared* ignore him.

He hadn't forgotten the Viennese Jews, whom he blamed for ruining his artistic career. Within days of his entry, "Hangman" Heydrich arrived with his Gestapo and SS action units. Jewish men and women were rounded up and made to clean public toilets with their bare hands; others scrubbed the streets on their hands and knees. Wealthier Jews were encouraged to buy their way out of Austria by giving their businesses and property to the Nazis. About one hundred thousand people, half of Austria's Jews, left in this way. Although penniless, they were the lucky ones. The others would soon be swallowed up in the Holocaust.

The fall of Austria put Hitler in position to gobble up yet another country, Czechoslovakia. Germany and Austria bordered this democratic republic on three sides in the west.

The triumphant return. Hitler enjoys his victory parade through the streets of Vienna in 1938.

Although a Slavic country, it had 3.5 million German-speaking citizens in the Sudetenland, an area taken from Austria in 1919. When Hitler took power, thousands of these people, aided by German Nazis, formed the Czech Nazi Party to demand that the Sudetenland be given to the Third Reich.

Der Fuehrer agreed. He ordered the Czech Nazis to hold disorderly demonstrations to provoke the police to violence against "peace-loving Germans." Dr. Goebbels took up the cry with newspaper headlines about "Czech Atrocities!"

Hitler made his move in September 1938, demanding that Czechoslovakia surrender the Sudetenland or face war with Germany. Yet the Sudetenland was just a cover for a complete takeover. He hoped that losing this valuable territory would so weaken Czechoslovakia that the government would collapse. Control of Czechoslovakia would allow him to menace his next victim, Poland, from the south. The German portion of that country also included the Skoda Works, one of the world's leading makers of big guns and tanks.

The Czechs refused to see their country torn apart. The government, confident of Allied support, announced it would fight for Czech freedom. Even Hitler's generals feared that he had gone too far this time.

But *der Fuehrer* counted on his gamble paying off once again. And why not? The Allied leaders—"little worms," he called them—had let him get away with the Rhineland and Austria. Surely his luck would hold a third time. It did.

British Prime Minister Neville Chamberlain and French Premier Édouard Daladier thought twice about helping Czechoslovakia. "Is the Sudetenland worth another war?"

they asked themselves. The answer always came back a ringing "No!"

During the last two days of September 1938, Chamberlain and Daladier met Hitler and Italian dictator Benito Mussolini for a conference at Munich; Czechoslovakia wasn't invited. They decided that the Sudetenland had to be given up for the sake of European peace; otherwise Czechoslovakia would have to fight on its own.

Everything went as Hitler planned. Crippled by the loss of the Sudetenland, Czechoslovakia was invaded by her neighbors. Within six months, Hungary and Poland grabbed thousands of square miles of territory to the north and south. The government collapsed, and the Czech Nazis took over Prague, the capital. On March 15, 1939, the German army swarmed across the border without firing a shot.

Hitler was overjoyed. "Children," he cried to his secretaries, "this is the greatest day of my life! I shall go down in history as the greatest German of all time!"

Millions of Germans agreed. He had restored their pride as a nation and they were grateful. Some Hitler jokes drew smiles even from the Gestapo. It was said, for example, that the army would give him a fiftieth birthday present: movable frontier posts.

The democracies, in the meantime, were becoming nervous. Hitler's victories had been easy—*too* easy. They had to draw the line before he pounced on his next victim, Poland. During the spring of 1939, Great Britain and France promised to declare war if he attacked Poland.

Hitler ignored their warning. He had scores to settle with Poland, a military dictatorship, and would settle them whatever the democracies did. The seaport of Danzig (now Gdansk) and other German territory had been given to Poland at the end of the First World War. The Fuehrer, like most Germans, wanted these lands back and was ready to fight for them. But unlike his countrymen, he wanted more. As with the Sudetenland, he was using these lands as an excuse for conquest. His true aim was the annihilation of Poland.

Hitler laid his plans carefully. In case the democracies honored their pledge, he had to finish off Poland quickly and shift his armies westward. In order to do this, he had to make a deal with Soviet leader Joseph Stalin.

"Uncle Joe" Stalin was a brutal tyrant who'd murdered millions of Russians in the name of Communism. Stalin knew that the Red Army was no match for the Wehrmacht. To gain time to expand his forces, he signed a treaty (August 23, 1939) in which he agreed to join Germany in the event of a war with Poland. This Nazi-Soviet pact was Poland's death warrant.

Hitler summoned his generals to announce his decision. War was certain. He'd already signed the necessary orders. German forces were secretly massing along the Polish border, ready down to the last polished button and the last bullet. Before the generals left to join their units, he gave them a final order. With a harsh, dry voice, his eyes blazing, *der Fuehrer* said, "Close your hearts to pity! . . . The stronger man is right. . . . Be harsh and remorseless! Be steeled against all signs of compassion." It was their duty to be cruel.

At 0445 hours (4:45 A.M.), Friday, September 1, 1939, 1.5 million German soldiers supported by 3,000 tanks and 1,600 planes burst across the Polish border. After waiting two days, Great Britain and France honored their pledges to Poland.

Hitler was with his henchmen when news of the Allies' action came. Everyone sat silently for a moment, realizing that nothing would ever again be the same for themselves and the world. At last Luftwaffe commander Hermann Goering broke the silence with these words: "If we lose this war, may Heaven have mercy upon us!"

The Second World War had begun.

Hitler had learned much from the mistakes of the First World War. He and his generals remembered how armies had bogged down in the trenches for four and a half years. The lesson: In the future, Germany's armies must move faster. They must move *through* the enemy, *around* him, and *over* him. They must use swarms of tanks and planes to make *Blitzkrieg*, "lightning war."

Blitzkrieg was war such as the world had never seen. Its rules were summarized in three words: surprise, force, speed. And Poland became the model for blitzkrieg copied in a dozen countries within two years.*

Hitler did not believe in "gentlemanly" warfare. Time-honored rules of warfare meant nothing to him. He would attack suddenly, without a declaration of war. He would hit first, hit hard, and keep on hitting until the enemy surrendered or died.

Before sunrise, September 1, the sky west of the Polish border was lit up by a false dawn. Thousands of gunflashes created an eerie light, followed by a deep rumbling. High-explosive shells began falling on their frontier outposts and

---

*The other blitzkrieg victims were France, Belgium, the Netherlands, Luxembourg, Norway, Denmark, Greece, Yugoslavia, Latvia, Lithuania, Estonia, and the U.S.S.R.

the Poles knew they were at war. The ground shook. Great domes of earth leaped upward, carrying stones, trees, and pieces of men.

But surprise attack was only the beginning of blitzkrieg. At sunrise planes roared down scores of Luftwaffe runways. Their mission was to tear up the enemy's rear areas, spreading panic among civilians and confusion among the military. Every target had been pinpointed on maps weeks earlier. Every plane had its own assignment. Every mission was part of a vast jigsaw puzzle, Hitler's plan for conquest.

Formations of two-engined Heinkel bombers pounded Polish communications: rail yards, bridges, road junctions, radio stations, telegraph lines, highways. Swarms of sleek Messerschmitt-109 fighters patrolled above the bombers, their guns hot for Polish aircraft. Few appeared.

Most of Poland's air force was destroyed on the ground in the war's first hours. Every airfield was struck and struck hard. Polish airmen learned about the war when a high-pitched scream came from overhead. Looking up, they saw Stukas, dive-bombers, plummeting toward them in a nearly straight line. The Stukas had sirens attached to their wing tips; Hitler believed that the sound would terrify people on the ground, and he was right.

Bombs plowed runways and smashed rows of parked airplanes. Hangars, control towers, fuel tanks, and ammunition dumps became heaps of flaming rubble. Those planes not destroyed on the ground were shot down by the faster and better-armed Messerschmitts. Shooting them down was often easier than Luftwaffe training exercises.

In the meantime, the panzers began to roll. *Panzer* is German for "armor," and armor meant tanks. All military powers had tank forces that were used in much the same way. Ever since their invention during the First World War, tanks had been sent into battle individually or in small groups to protect the foot soldiers. The Germans, however, changed the rules, making tanks the backbone of blitzkrieg. When Hitler came to power, he ordered the creation of entire panzer divisions, each a small, fast-moving army on wheels.

The panzer division was a battle division. Instead of supporting foot soldiers, it was to strike the enemy like a gigantic sledgehammer. It had plenty of force to do the job. Each panzer division had about 300 tanks, plus hundreds of armored cars, antiaircraft guns, and antitank guns that fired armor-piercing shells timed to explode inside an enemy tank. SP—self-propelled guns—were heavy cannon that raced along under their own power at forty miles an hour. In addition, thousands of panzer grenadiers, or mobile infantry, traveled in armored troop carriers.

The panzer division's fighters were supported by thousands of other men and machines. Rolling repair shops fixed most tank breakdowns in a few hours. Engineer units bridged streams and filled bomb craters in roads to keep the panzers moving at top speed. Truck convoys brought supplies, especially fuel; a panzer division in combat needed a thousand gallons of gasoline per *mile* on good roads, twice that when crossing open fields. Communications trucks carried the division's radios and Enigma, Germany's secret machine for coding and decoding messages.

Artillery shells were still falling when Polish soldiers heard the chugging of heavy engines and the clatter and clang of steel treads. Curiosity turned to terror when they saw hundreds of ten- and twenty-ton tanks coming at them at once.

Armored battering rams broke the Polish lines at the

weakest points. The panzers smashed through barbed-wire barricades, then rolled over the trenches they were supposed to protect. Machine-gun nests were simply crushed into a mess of twisted iron, torn cloth, and bloody earth. Fleeing men were overtaken from behind and flattened.

Polish machine-gunners firing from houses were amazed at the enemy's response. Tankers revved their motors and rammed the houses at twenty-five miles an hour. Walls collapsed. Roofs caved in amid clouds of dust. Satisfied that the machine guns were silenced, the tankers backed out of the ruins and kept moving.

That was the panzers' mission: to keep moving, *fast!* Whenever possible, they avoided Polish strongpoints such as forts and towns. Strongpoints were bypassed, like a stream flowing around boulders. The idea was to keep the enemy off balance by driving wedges between his forces and preventing them from acting together. The faster the panzers moved, the harder they were to locate and counterattack.

A panzer division was a well-oiled killing machine. The moment it met resistance it couldn't bypass, say a line of concrete pillboxes, the tanks halted. There was a whirring of motors as the big turrets swung into position.

Bam!

Tatatatatatata.

Tanks poured cannon and machine-gun fire into the defenders. Self-propelled guns lobbed shells from the distance. Panzer grenadiers, many armed with flamethrowers, moved to the attack. Soon the Polish positions were drenched in high explosives and fire. The air reeked of burned gunpowder and gasoline.

If the defenders still held on, the panzer leader, usually

a general, ordered "special treatment": he called in an air strike.

Soon the flying artillery, the Stukas, were blasting the area with 110-pound bombs. Some pilots were so skilled that it was said they could put a bomb into a pickle barrel from two thousand feet. Messerschmitts came in at treetop level, raking the enemy with machine-gun bullets. The blockage cleared, the panzers sprang forward again.

They were followed by the main body of the German army. These forces, slower-moving but larger and with heavier equipment, attacked bypassed strongpoints and occupied the conquered territory. Their every move had been thought out in advance and carefully planned.

Among the forces Hitler sent into Poland were divisions of the Weapons SS. Unlike the regular army in their gray-green uniforms, the Weapons SS wore black from head to toe. Fanatical Nazis, they were feared even by fellow German soldiers.

The training of the Weapons SS was made so difficult that battle would seem easy by comparison. Trainees were made to fight German police dogs to test their courage and ability to think quickly. As soon as the cages were opened, the dogs, snarling brutes with fiery eyes and bared fangs, leaped at the men's throats. Without protection, they had to overcome the dogs barehanded. Nobody helped them if they had serious trouble.

Endurance tests in the Weapons SS were for keeps; if you failed, you died. A squad of rookies were given shovels and sent into an open field. Across the way stood tanks with their motors running. An instructor blew his whistle, and the men began to dig. After five minutes, the tanks raced toward the squad and over its foxholes. If your foxhole wasn't deep enough, you were ground to pieces beneath the tanks' treads. Weapons SS officer cadets might have to pull the pin of a grenade, balance it on their helmets, and stand at attention as it exploded. If it was well-balanced, the explosion's force went upward, without harming the men.

Beginning in Poland, the Weapons SS earned a name for bravery, toughness, and cruelty. Prisoners were often shot. If a sniper fired at SS men from a building, the town might be burned to the ground and its people massacred. Women and children were not spared.

The blitzkrieg rolled across Poland day after day. Nature itself seemed to favor the invaders. Instead of late-summer rains turning the fields to mud, they enjoyed "Hitler weather." Intense sun baked the Polish plains concrete-hard, allowing the panzers to travel at top speed. Every evening, as the sun set like a red saucer, Nazi officers shaded in another part of the conquered country on their maps.

Poles went into battle singing their national anthem:

. . . *as long as we live*
Poland shall not die.

Outnumbered and outsmarted, lacking planes and modern equipment, the Poles fought their losing battle. Often they fought recklessly, sacrificing their lives to save their country's honor. Cavalry regiments, relics of a bygone age, charged massed machine guns. It was breathtaking to watch thousands of men charging across the fields on splendid horses, their swords raised and glinting in the sun. But it wasn't war. The Germans cut them down by the hundreds without losing a man. Cavalry sometimes attacked tanks. Horses against steel. Swords against cannon. But raw courage wasn't enough to stop Hitler's steamroller.

Hitler followed every detail of the campaign, going everywhere with his maps and demanding that officers explain what was going on in great detail. Passing troops were amazed to see him scrambling over a wrecked Polish armored train with a tape measure; he was calculating the distances between bomb craters on either side in order to suggest better dive-bombing methods for the Luftwaffe. Hitler visited German wounded in hospitals, even had lunch with troops bound for the front. The men were thrilled at their Fuehrer's interest and greeted him with rousing choruses of "We're Marching on Poland" and shouts of *"Heil Hitler!"* whenever he appeared.

Yet for those he attacked, Hitler had no sympathy. He remarked during the bombing of Warsaw that Poles were uncivilized for not surrendering and making him punish them so severely. It never occurred to him that, perhaps, he was doing them an injustice. Anything he did was right, in his own eyes.

Poland was already defeated when Stalin invaded from the east on September 17. That was the final blow. Caught between Germany and Russia, Poland surrendered two days later. Eastern Poland, about one third of the country, went to Russia; Hitler took the rest, including Warsaw, the capital.

When Warsaw surrendered, a Polish general met General Erich von Manstein, the local German commander. Manstein was very "proper" and polite. As he reached out to shake the Pole's hand, the man said, "The

wheel always turns full circle." One day, he knew, Hitler's
legions would taste the bitterness of defeat.

Lightning war in the east was followed by the "Phony War"
in the west, lasting from October 1939 to April 1940. These
six months are called the Phony War because Great Britain,
France, and Germany didn't fight, even though they'd become enemies.

Hitler's armies returned from Poland to man defenses
opposite France. France mobilized her armies. The BEF
(British Expeditionary Force) crossed the English Channel
and took positions in northern France, along the border
with Belgium. Belgium, though neutral, called up its reserves, just in case.

Like Hitler, the Allies learned from the mistakes of the
First World War, only the lessons they learned were quite
different. Never again would they send men to be slaughtered in the open by the millions. They planned instead to
stay on the defensive, letting the Germans waste their strength
in costly attacks. Allied defenses were strong, and they felt
safe behind them.

During the 1930s France had built the Maginot Line to
keep out German invaders. Named after War Minister André
Maginot, this line of underground forts stretched from
Switzerland to the Belgian border. It was as if hundreds of
battleships had been buried beneath twenty feet of concrete,
allowing only their gun turrets to show. Each fortress had
everything needed for defense: underground barracks, mess
halls, hospitals, power stations, telephone exchanges, ammunition dumps. Underground railways sped troops and
supplies to their destinations.

Every foot of ground facing Germany was noted on fire control plans, saving Maginot Line gunners valuable time in aiming. Even single bushes and trees were targeted. No one could set foot in the defense zone without meeting death from a dozen directions.

The Belgian defenses seemed equally strong. In the south, along the French-Luxembourgian-German border, lay the Ardennes country with its steep hills, thick forests, and narrow roads. Allied planners believed it impossible to move masses of men and armor through this rugged area.

North of the Ardennes lay the Meuse River and Albert Canal, forming the border with the Netherlands. Belgian troops had mined the bridges over these vital waterways and could destroy them in seconds. Fort Eben Emael, the largest fortress ever built, overlooked the spot where the waterways joined. Allied experts believed that the Germans would need a whole army and at least a week to capture Eben Emael. Even if they succeeded, the time wasted would allow the Allies to prepare their counterattacks.

Hitler let the Allies huddle inside their fortresses, while he planned a super blitzkrieg. The Phony War ended suddenly on April 9, 1940, when his armies crashed into Denmark and Norway. Both countries were important as air and naval bases for an assault on Great Britain.

Surprise was complete. Denmark, a small country on Germany's northern border, fell in a day. Her army of 14,000, smaller than one panzer division, was no match for German armor and aircraft. Rather than see his troops slaughtered, King Christian X ordered them to give up.

The Norwegian invasion went like clockwork. Within twelve hours Oslo, the capital, fell into German hands, along with the nation's major seaports. Luftwaffe transports simply landed troops at Oslo Airport. The troops easily overwhelmed the defenders and took over the capital. Warships boldly steamed into Norwegian ports with cargoes of troops and light tanks.

The Norwegians fought back as best they could. Although fighting dragged on for nearly a month, German control of their country was never really threatened after the invasion day. The takeover was aided by traitors in the Norwegian military and by the Norwegian branch of the Nazi Party. Major Vidkun Quisling, a former defense minister and a leading Nazi, gave the invaders key secrets. Quisling paid for his crime before a firing squad after Norway's liberation in 1945.

Hitler's next blow came swiftly and where least expected. Clearly it would be suicide to attack the Maginot Line head-on. He and his generals decided that the blow must fall not in the center of the French defenses, but to the north, where they ended.

Two huge armies, stiffened by ten panzer divisions, were secretly gathered opposite Belgium, Luxembourg, and Holland. The plan was to break through at key points in these countries and then lunge into France herself. Once in the open, the panzers would race crosscountry. Some would turn right, north, toward the English Channel, trapping the BEF. The rest would speed southward, *behind* the Maginot Line, toward Paris and the French heartland.

Before dawn, Friday, May 10, 1940, people awakened to the sound of rattling windows and the droning of engines overhead. Peering into the half-darkness, they saw the sky filled with planes. Wave upon wave of German bombers

were heading west. Without a word friend and foe knew
that Hitler was on the march again.

Among the aircraft were three-motored Junker transports,
some with paratroops, others towing gliders at the end of
steel cables. The airborne part of the invasion was *der Fuehrer's* own idea. The paratroops had trained for it on bridges
in Germany and on an exact model of Fort Eben Emael.
Their mission: clear the way over the Meuse River and
Albert Canal for the panzers. If they failed, the entire campaign might fail. Handpicked men, they would rather
have died than shamed themselves by disappointing their
leader.

As the transports dived, leveling off at 600 feet above the
ground, the paratroops jumped head-first. Jumping from
600 feet is asking for trouble; only daredevil performers jump
so close to the ground. Scores of Germans died when their
parachutes failed to open completely, or when they fell into
the Meuse. Most, however, came down safely. Belgians
guarding the three largest bridges were overpowered before
they could detonate the mines. Already the panzers were
on their way.

At about the same time, three gliders skidded to a stop
on Fort Eben Emael's concrete roof. Eighty-five paratroop-
engineers scrambled out and began attacking the 1,200 men
in the fortress beneath their feet.

The Germans were so well-trained that every action came
automatically. Moving quickly, they dynamited the barrels
of the giant guns. Explosives were tossed into the ventilating
system, shaking the fortress and filling its chambers with
smoke. Hatches were blown open, and flamethrower nozzles poked through. Early next morning, the "impregnable"

Fort Eben Emael surrendered. The way across Belgium was open.

Far to the north, tank columns were lancing through Holland. Nothing was allowed to stand in their way or slow them down. Opposition was buried under tank treads and bombs. The port city of Rotterdam was destroyed in a single air raid that killed nearly a thousand civilians and left seventy-eight thousand homeless. On the fourth day, May 14, the Dutch surrendered and the panzers crossed the river barrier into Belgium. Turning right, northward, they dashed for the English Channel and its vital seaports.

German armor, in the meantime, roared across Luxembourg and began doing the "impossible." Thousands of tanks and other vehicles jammed the roads of the Ardennes. The few Allied troops in the area were easily brushed aside or blasted by the Luftwaffe.

Reaching open country, the panzers turned south. They raced past Sedan, Toul, Château-Thierry, Belleau Wood, and a hundred other places familiar to the American doughboys of 1917–1918. The millions of francs spent on the Maginot Line didn't even buy a day. The invaders simply passed behind the concrete-covered battleships on their way to Paris.

The Allies met a new breed of German soldier in 1940, a man who'd been shaped by the Hitler Youth. He was not what they'd expected, a man like themselves serving his country, but a fanatic. A wounded prisoner was told by a French doctor that he needed a blood transfusion. The prisoner replied angrily, "I will not have my German blood polluted with French blood. I would rather die." And he did.

Another dying Nazi was offered last rites by a priest. "The Fuehrer is my faith," he cried. "I don't want anything from your church. But if you want to be good to me, get my Fuehrer's picture out of my breast pocket." The priest did as requested. "My Fuehrer, I am happy to die for you," said the soldier, kissing the picture.

The Germans used every means to keep up the pressure. Towns in rear areas were bombed, not to hit military targets, but to drive the people from their homes. French men and women, young and old, crowded the roads seeking safety. People walked, rode bicycles, drove farm wagons, or inched along in overheating cars. The sick and exhausted lay panting in ditches or under trees. All had terror in their eyes.

Suddenly bloodcurdling noises came from overhead. Stukas!

Dive-bombers swooped low over the refugees, machine guns chattering. No mistake; they meant to shoot helpless civilians. It was all part of a plan to herd them along certain roads, where they'd disrupt French reinforcements and supplies bound for the front.

French resistance crumbled. Entire regiments panicked, threw away their weapons, and ran. Fear was contagious, infecting one outfit after another. Even professional officers lost hope.

French President Paul Reynaud received a postcard found on the body of an officer who'd committed suicide. He wrote: "I am killing myself, Mr. President, to let you know that my men were brave, but one cannot send men to fight tanks with rifles."

The tanks kept coming. By the end of May, the BEF, plus French and Belgian units, were trapped with their back to the English Channel. The Germans had taken all the nearby ports except Dunkirk, a small city in the northeastern corner of France. Unless the British acted immediately, the BEF, which included nearly the whole of their peacetime army, would be wiped out. If that happened, a defenseless Britain would have to make peace on Hitler's terms. It would be the end of liberty in Europe.

During the evening of May 26, Winston Churchill, Prime Minister for only two weeks, gave one of the most important orders of the Second World War: "Begin Operation Dynamo." Dynamo was the codeword for the emergency plan to evacuate the BEF. For the next nine days, Dunkirk held the center of the world's attention.

The Germans had Dunkirk surrounded by an ever-tightening ring of steel and fire. The city was a shambles of ruined buildings and rubble-strewn streets. Blazing oil tanks along the waterfront sent plumes of flame and sooty smoke into the sky. The harbor was choked with wrecked ships, and the docks were useless. Troops could be evacuated only from a long breakwater jutting into the Channel from the harbor's mouth and off a strip of beach to the east.

Dynamo began to pick up speed. Down the creeks of England's South Coast, out of dockyards and harbors and tiny coves, came "the little boats." It was a people's armada, sent by a seafaring nation to rescue its sons. Every type of private boat put to sea when the evacuation order came. There were ferries, paddle steamers, sailing yachts, speedboats, motorized lifeboats, even tugs pulling strings of barges. The conquered nations were represented by vessels that had escaped the Germans in the nick of time: Dutch schuits, Norwegian merchantmen, Danish and French fishing boats.

The miracle of Dunkirk. With Hitler's armies closing in, thousands of British and French soldiers patiently wait their turn to be rescued from the beaches of Dunkirk.

This strange fleet was manned by merchant sailors and office clerks, dentists, butchers, taxi drivers, and bright-eyed Sea Scouts. Supporting them were units of the Royal Navy, minesweepers and destroyers bristling with guns.

There was no need to plot a course. A skipper had only to head into the English Channel and steer for the smoke rising in the distance. That was Dunkirk.

Along the way they passed homeward-bound vessels packed with tired, bedraggled men in khaki. These men didn't act like the remnants of a beaten army. Many cheered and gave the thumbs-up salute to the passing vessels. Although defeated, their spirits remained unbroken. They were still fighting men.

Nearing the French coast, the rescuers passed through miles of floating wreckage and, too often, khaki-clad bodies bobbing in the calm sea. It was like sailing into a shooting gallery, with yourself as the target. Messerschmitts darted overhead, iron hawks stalking their prey. Geysers erupted among the ships as large-caliber shells and bombs exploded in the sea.

Royal Navy warships lay offshore, sending up flaming curtains of antiaircraft fire. Their five-inch guns dropped shells inland, seeking out the panzers.

Sailors saw long, brown lines on the Dunkirk breakwater and snaking along the beach. These were men, thousands upon thousands of British Tommies, French *poilus*, and Belgian *soldats*. Since Dunkirk's docks were unusable, the larger ships had to anchor outside the harbor, making their passengers come out to them. Men waited on the breakwater for a place in a small boat to ferry them to a vessel for the cross-Channel voyage. Others stood up to their shoulders in the surf off the sandy beach. After they were hauled into the boats, comrades in the rear moved up from knee-deep to waist-deep to shoulder-deep waters until their turn came. Often that took many hours.

In the meantime, "Jerry," as they nicknamed the Germans, threw everything he had at them. Long-range guns peppered the columns with shrapnel, steel splinters that could slice a person in half. Fighters zipped over the columns, bombing and machine-gunning everything in sight.

All the troops could do was stand their ground, shoot back with rifles, and pray—*hard*. The beach was littered with wounded, whose "mates" cared for them any way they could. The dead were left where they fell, unburied. Burned-out trucks, smashed cannon, and wrecked planes were everywhere. Most of these planes had swastikas on their tails.

When Dynamo ended on June 4, 1940, some 218,000 British and 120,000 French and Belgian troops were saved. Left behind were 68,000 men of the BEF, killed or captured, and all their equipment. But machines are only things; they can be replaced. Saving the men, that was the true miracle of Dunkirk. The survivors would soon become the core of a new army that would in time help to bury the Third Reich.

That evening, as the last boats came home, Winston Churchill spoke to the British people. Churchill at sixty-five was a ruby-cheeked, heavy-set man who liked good food, good whiskey, and good cigars. As a young man, he'd served with the British army in India and as a reporter in wars from Cuba to South Africa. Stubborn and proud, generous and fearless, "Winnie" was more than a match for Adolf Hitler.

Churchill didn't try to sugarcoat the facts. He told the

truth, the plain, harsh truth. Wars aren't won by evacuations. Things were bad and would get worse. Yet the British had always been a free people, and they weren't about to change now. They'd never surrender. Never. With Dunkirk's flames visible from the white cliffs of Dover, the Prime Minister promised:

> We shall not flag or fail. We shall go on to the end. We shall fight . . . on the seas and oceans. We shall fight . . . in the air. We shall defend our island whatever the cost may be. We shall fight on the beaches. We shall fight on the landing grounds. We shall fight in the fields and in the streets. We shall fight in the hills. We shall never surrender. . . .

Paris fell on June 14, 1940, ten days after Dynamo ended. What Imperial Germany couldn't do in the four and a half years of the First World War, Hitler's panzers did in a month.

The Battle of France was over.

The Battle of Britain was about to begin.

Hitler's taste for battle grew with his victories. Just weeks after the fall of France, he set his planners to work on Operation Sea Lion, the invasion of Great Britain. Soon Nazi armies were massing along the coast from France to Norway. Shipping was gathered, and the Luftwaffe built bases as close as possible to their target. "Hangman" Heydrich chose the Gestapo units that would police the island nation for the Fuehrer. Lists were made of Englishmen marked for immediate arrest and execution; sites were selected for concentration camps outside London.

DER FUEHRER *celebrates the fall of France with a little dance. This is one of the few pictures that show Hitler with a broad grin on his face.*

The British knew what to expect and prepared for the worst. Factories worked around the clock to replace the equipment lost at Dunkirk. A million men too old for military service joined the Home Guard to patrol the coasts; often their only weapons were ancient shotguns and spears. Trenches were dug and barbed wire strung along beaches. Concrete pillars sprouted like mushrooms in country fields and city parks to prevent glider landings. Key factories, bridges, and other targets were protected by barrage balloons, huge gas-filled bags flown on steel cables to snare low-flying planes.

Britain's first line of defense, its priceless treasure, was the RAF, the Royal Air Force. Both sides knew that the Battle of Britain would be won or lost in the sky. Hitler couldn't move without control of the air over the English Channel and the invasion beaches. Although only twenty-one miles wide at its narrowest point, the English Channel seemed like an ocean to the Nazis. As long as the RAF had enough planes and pilots, it could sink any force that tried to cross from the Continent. Better still, it could cover the British fleet, still one of the strongest on earth, allowing it to sweep the seas of enemy shipping.

It was up to the RAF pilots, mostly men in their early twenties, to keep control of the sky over the sea. It was a big job. On the eve of the Battle of Britain, July 1940, the Luftwaffe had a first-line bombing fleet of 1,480 planes, with hundreds more in reserve. These were short-range, lightly armed aircraft designed for close support of the panzers. Even if they could reach distant targets, they would be sitting ducks without fighter escorts. Hitler allowed 980 fighters for the campaign, mostly Messerschmitt-109s. The

ME-109 was fast (357 miles an hour), easy to handle, and packed a terrific punch in its two machine guns and two small, quick-firing cannon. German pilots were veteran air-fighters used to winning. They'd made mincemeat of their opponents and expected to do so once again. One of their favorite songs was "Bombs on England":

> Listen to the engine singing—
>   get on to the foe!
> Listen, in your ears it's ringing—
>   get on to the foe!
> BOMBS, OH BOMBS ON ENGLAND!

RAF Fighter Command had 591 planes at the beginning of the battle, mostly Hurricanes and "Spits"—Spitfires. These carried eight machine guns and at 362 miles an hour were slightly faster than the Messerschmitts. The Hurricane was a sturdy, reliable plane, but the Spitfire was a pilot's dream. It could outclimb the ME-109, stay with it in the tightest turns, and was easier for ground crews to service.

In mid-August 1940, Hitler unleashed the full fury of the Luftwaffe. Objective: the RAF. RAF airfields, repair shops, and fuel dumps were to be destroyed in preparation for Sea Lion. It would be a duel of eagles. When it ended, Winston Churchill would praise RAF Fighter Command in an im-mortal saying: "Never in the field of human conflict was so much owed by so many to so few."

A fighter action began long before raiders flew over the English Channel. Surprise attacks were rare, since Fighter Command knew when the enemy was coming, sometimes even his exact target. The British were masters at "wizard's war," the use of science in warfare. Their scientists had learned the secrets of the Enigma machine, and that gave them an important advantage. British decoders could read every Luftwaffe message, so that Churchill often had Fuehrer orders on his desk before they reached German air fleets at their bases.

Equally important were the mysterious 350-foot towers along the English coast. These were the first radar stations, another British invention. As soon as enemy planes took off, they were detected by radio waves beamed from the towers. The planes' number, course, altitude, and speed were monitored until they swept over the English coast. Once the planes were over England, ground-spotters took over from the radar stations during daylight. Thousands of men and women had been trained to follow enemy movements once the enemy flew inland. This was important, because early warning meant lives to the defenders.

Radar and ground-spotter reports poured into Fighter Command control centers by telephone, where they were noted on large maps set out on tables. The maps were covered with tiny airplane models representing invading and defending forces. The models were constantly moved, giving at a glance an exact situation report from minute to minute.

The system's success depended upon women. British women not only took jobs in factories, replacing men drafted into the services, they actually joined in the air battles of 1940. Most radar operators were women. Women in RAF uniform plotted the raiders' course on the control center maps. Women antiaircraft gunners shot them down in flames. Women stayed at their posts near flaming gasoline tanks, pulled pilots from wrecked planes, and died at their guns.

As the raiders passed through the black puffs of exploding antiaircraft shells, sirens wailed at Fighter Command bases. Squadrons were kept grounded until the last moment to save fuel and increase flight time in combat. This was a valuable advantage, since German fighters had come so far that they could stay over most targets only fifteen minutes before having to turn back. Any delay meant running out of fuel and crash-landing in England or "the Sewer," their name for the English Channel. Bombers often went on to targets without fighter protection.

Loudspeakers blared, "Squadrons up! Scramble, scramble, SCRAMBLE!"

The airfields were a flurry of action as pilots ran to their planes. Engines sputtered and coughed. Propellers spun. Planes sped down runways four or five at a time. Soon they were airborne and climbing.

Ambush was the fighter pilot's game. He lived (or died) by three simple rules:

> He who has height controls the battle.
> He who has the sun achieves surprise.
> He who gets in close shoots them down.

The British cruised above twenty thousand feet; the higher you flew, the faster you could dive at a lower-flying enemy. Positioning yourself with your back to the sun made you invisible to an enemy below. Swooping down from the sun and firing at close range, from thirty to one hundred feet, usually meant a kill. Five kills and you became an "ace," one of the bravest of the brave.

When Nazi formations appeared, the British squadron leaders gave the foxhunters' call over their radios: "Tallyho!"

Instantly Hurricanes and Spitfires peeled off to the right or left and dived. Engines whined as they came down under full power. Machine guns chattered.

"*Achtung, Schpitfeure!*"—"Attention, Spitfires!"—Germans shouted into their radios when they saw the danger. Breaking formation, the ME-109s left the bombers to care for themselves. While some Spitfires pounced on the bombers, the others began a no-holds-barred dogfight with their escorts.

A dogfight was a swirl of movement. Things happened quickly, and for keeps. Planes flashed by each other, twisting, turning, diving, zooming straight up to charge an enemy head-on. Pilots, misjudging speed or distance, crashed into each other or slammed into the ground. Planes spun out of control, trailing banners of flame. Planes exploded with a loud *whuff*, disintegrating in showers of red-hot metal. Airmen hurtled earthward, their parachutes aflame.

D. M. Crook of the RAF 609th Squadron told how it felt to shoot a man down over the English Channel:

> At that moment I saw dimly a machine moving in cloud on my left and flying parallel to me. I stalked him through the cloud and when he emerged into a patch of clear sky, I saw that it was a [Stuka]. I was in an ideal position to attack, and opened fire and put the remainder of my ammunition—about 2000 rounds—into him at very close range. Even in the heat of the moment I well remember my amazement at the shattering effect of my fire. Pieces flew off his fuselage and cockpit covering, a stream of smoke appeared from the engine, and a moment

later a great sheet of flame licked out from the engine
cowling and he dived down vertically. The flames
enveloped the whole machine and he went straight
down, apparently quite slowly, until he was just a
shapeless burning mass of wreckage. Absolutely fascinated by the sight, I followed him down and saw
him hit the sea with a great burst of white foam. He
disappeared immediately, and apart from a green
patch in the water there was no sign that anything
had happened. . . . I had often wondered what would
be my feelings when killing somebody like this, and
especially when seeing him go down in flame. . . . I
was rather surprised to reflect afterwards that my only
feeling had been one of considerable elation, and a
sort of bewildered surprise that it had been so easy.

Jerry came often that summer of 1940. He was fighting
the calendar as much as Fighter Command. Hitler had to
destroy the RAF before the fall, when storms would ruin
chances for a cross-Channel invasion.

August 15 and 18 were Luftwaffe "Eagle Days," when
upwards of 500 bombers and 1,000 fighters struck RAF
bases. Places like Kenley, Biggin Hill, Hornchurch, and
North Weald suddenly became vital to free people everywhere. Americans read about the air battles there as if they
were happening in the next town. Jerry came, and Churchill's young men shot him from the sky. The Luftwaffe
lost 143 planes in two days at a cost of 63 to the RAF.

Picnickers on those clear, balmy days lay on their backs
and watched dogfights overhead. White vapor trails curled
in the blue sky. From above came a sound like sticks run

quickly over picket fences: machine-gun fire. An English radio broadcaster described a Stuka falling in flames for his audience:

> There's one coming down in flames—there's a long streak—he's coming down completely out of control—a long streak of smoke—ah, a man's bailed out by parachute—the pilot's bailed out by parachute—he's a Junkers 87 and he's going slap into the sea and there he goes—sma-a-ash. . . . Oh boy, I've never seen anything so good as this—the RAF fighters have really got those boys [sized-up].

Hitler drove his airmen onward, ignoring losses. By the end of August, his determination was paying off. Fighter Command was nearing collapse. Although British aircraft production soared, pilots could not be manufactured on assembly lines. Many had died or were lying in hospitals, crippled. Everyone else was exhausted. Men would fly six missions a day until they "cracked up," had nervous breakdowns. Another week and Fighter Command would be finished.

Der Fuehrer knew he was winning. Already he'd ordered the Gestapo to prepare lists of English people to be arrested the moment the nation surrendered. Some, like the royal family, would be kept as puppets, provided they obeyed their Nazi masters. But most politicians, military leaders, clergymen, and journalists would be sent to concentration camps to be built in the English countryside. All Jews would be rounded up and, in the Nazis' say-nothing language, "dealt with by appropriate means."

Hitler would have won had he kept up the pressure a

little longer. Luckily Churchill, like a good fisherman, put
out some bait for "the greatest German of all time." When
a German squadron bombed London by mistake, Churchill
used this as an excuse to bomb Berlin. The German capital
was raided several times, causing minor damage. Hitler,
like a hungry fish, took the bait hook, line, and sinker. He
became furious, vowing revenge against British cities, especially London. "If they attack our cities, we will simply
rub out theirs," he swore.

This was his first big error of the war, for the moment
he switched from bombing airfields to bombing cities, he
took the pressure off Fighter Command and ruined Sea
Lion.

The air war against British cities is called "the Blitz."
From September 1940 to May 1941, one city after another
was "blitzed" without mercy. Raids became so bad that
Churchill ordered children evacuated. There were tearful
goodbyes as millions of youngsters boarded trains and buses
to the country, where they were taken in by foster families.
The Blitz gave many city children the opportunity to see
farms and cows for the first time in their lives.

London suffered more than any other city. Hitler took a
personal interest in the British capital. He wanted to make
it an example of what happened to those who defied the
Third Reich. He'd punish London for raids on Berlin and
break the spirit of its people so they'd force Churchill to
make peace on his terms.

Beginning September 7, and for the next seventy-five
days,* the Luftwaffe hammered London without letup. At

---

*They missed only one day, when bad weather forced cancellation of a raid.

first the bombers came in daylight, but when Fighter Command shot them down in droves, they switched to night attacks. Night bombing was less accurate, but safer.

Fighter Command's pilots, brave as they were, were not the heroes of the Blitz. They at least could fight back, returning the enemy bullet for bullet. But the civilians were up against a foe they couldn't harm. The Blitz became a battle of ordinary folk against a mighty war machine. On the front lines were rescue workers, ambulance drivers, telephone operators, policemen, doctors, nurses, firemen. Remember the firemen; they saved London. Without their courage and dedication, Europe's largest city would have become a pile of ashes in a week.

Air raids became the Londoners' way of life. First there were wailing sirens announcing that Hitler's bombers were coming. People knew what to do without being ordered. Civil defense workers rushed to their posts. Citizens took shelter wherever they could. Those who preferred to remain at home went into basements or hid under staircases, away from windows and flying glass; many had Andersons, small iron shelters buried in their gardens. Thousands of others went to the Underground, the deep railroad tunnels that wind for miles beneath London.

For those above ground, an air raid was a time of wonder and horror. The city was completely blacked out at night; streetlights were shut off, and it was a crime to show a light from a window. Even a flashlight could give German navigators a "fix" on the target. Unfortunately, the moon couldn't be put out; a full moon was called a "bombers' moon," and Londoners grew to hate it.

Sirens were still wailing when the first bombers soared

overhead. Suddenly crisscrossing searchlight beams stabbed cones of yellow light thousands of feet into the sky. Black shapes—planes—were seen moving across the light cones. The planes answered with lights of their own: parachute flares drifted down slowly, bathing London in a pale green light. It began.

Antiaircraft guns flashed and roared, sending shells streaming skyward. Every fifth shell was a "tracer" filled with a chemical that burned in the air, allowing gunners to see where their shots were going. Each gun battery had its own tracer color, so the sky soon lit up as in a fireworks show.

A plane exploded in an orange ball, scattering pieces of metal and men over the countryside below. Another plane, its gasoline tanks burst open, flew like a comet, trailing banners of flame and sparks.

Bombardiers pressed release buttons, unleashing a rain of death. Incendiaries were bottle-sized bombs filled with magnesium, which burns at a high temperature. High-explosive, or demolition, bombs weighed between one hundred and one thousand pounds. The heavier bombs had a blast so powerful that they could toss a man up from five blocks away and flick off his shoes and pants without harming him. Bomb fragments, slivers of glass, and chunks of stone flew through the air, deadly as bullets.

In the Underground, meantime, people huddled on the platforms, trying to sleep. It wasn't easy. Stations were crowded; one sheltered ten thousand people, and after each step you had to find a place to put your foot down without stepping on someone. Babies cried and wet their diapers. People snored, coughed, prayed, or sang to drown out the noise from above. Sometimes there were disasters, as when a bomb sliced through fifty feet of earth to explode inside a tunnel. Mostly, however, life in the Underground was safe, if nasty.

Life above ground was dangerous and nasty. Fire engines, ambulances, and rescue vehicles sped through the streets with sirens wailing. Buildings were collapsing all the time, and people had to be dug out of the rubble before they suffocated.

There were near-misses, some of which made rescuers chuckle. Like the time a lady shot down a flight of stairs and into the street in her bathtub. Or when a man was caught on the toilet when the side of his house collapsed.

But mostly it was rough going. Rescue workers struggled on, knowing a weakened wall might collapse on them at any moment. Firemen worked amid canyons of flame in narrow streets with every building burning on either side. Hungry and red-eyed with fatigue, they ate smoke, coughing as if their lungs would burst. Some blazes were so large, a reporter said, that "it looked just like little boys peeing on an enormous bonfire." A hundred million gallons of water might be used during a single air raid.

Churchill knew how people suffered and tried to raise their spirits. Often, after a raid, he had himself driven to the hardest-hit area. Stepping from the car, he walked the smoking, shattered streets accompanied only by a few policemen.

News of his arrival spread by word of mouth. People who'd just lost their homes, perhaps also loved ones, cheered their Prime Minister. "Good old Winnie," they'd shout, "you will never let us down." He'd make the V-for-victory sign with his fingers and call back, "Are we downhearted?" "No," came the reply, "London can take it."

And London *did* take it. On October 12, 1940, Hitler canceled Operation Sea Lion. The brave, defiant *Englaender* had handed the Fuehrer his first defeat.

The Battle of Britain was costly to both sides. RAF Fighter Command lost 1,017 planes and 537 pilots. Hitler lost 1,182 planes and 2,662 airmen. Civilians, however, suffered most. The Blitz took the lives of 43,000 people, of whom 30,000 were Londoners. Another 86,000 were badly injured. Yet these losses, terrible as they were, were small, compared with what the RAF and United States Army Air Force would later do to German cities in a single day.

Although the raids continued into the spring of 1941, the pressure gradually eased, and life began to return to normal. That spring Hitler began shifting forces for Operation Barbarossa, or "Redbeard." His order for Barbarossa was clear: "Russia must be liquidated. Spring 1941. The sooner Russia is smashed, the better."

BARBAROSSA

BEFORE DAWN ON JUNE 22, 1941, NAZI ARMIES WAITED IN darkness along a two-thousand-mile front from the Baltic Sea in the north to the Black Sea in the south. Across the border in Soviet-occupied Poland and in Russia herself, people slept peacefully, unaware of the storm that was about to break.

Hitler had always meant to attack Russia. It was all in *Mein Kampf*, where he explained that Germany needed "living space" in the East. Russians, in his twisted mind, were a race of *Untermenschen*, subhumans, without any rights whatsoever. In planning his attack, he passed a death sentence on an entire nation. Russia's cities were to be blasted to rubble. Her land and resources were to be taken by German settlers. Her people were to be driven from their homes and shot, starved, or worked to death as slaves.

The attack began in the usual blitzkrieg manner. There was no declaration of war, only the roar of artillery and the scream of Stukas. Surprise was total. "We are being fired on," a Russian unit radioed headquarters. "What shall we do?" Headquarters replied, "You must be insane. And why is your signal not in code?"

The Russians were surprised because of one man: Joseph Stalin. Stalin was a tyrant who ruled his country with an iron hand. His secret police, the NKVD, kept the country in terror. Anyone suspected of disloyalty or of not being a good Communist was executed or sent to the Gulag, slave labor camps in Siberia and the Arctic. It was at Stalin's command that over ten million farmers were killed when they objected to giving their property to the Communist government. Hitler both admired Stalin and hated him.

Stalin knew the exact date of the attack a month in advance. One of his spies, Richard Sorge, had been operating in Japan for eight years as a German newspaper correspondent. Sorge was friendly with Japanese officials and the German ambassador, who was kept informed of Hitler's plans. The moment Sorge learned of Operation Barbarossa, he radioed Moscow.

Stalin ignored the warning. This tyrant, suspicious of everyone around him, for some reason trusted Hitler. After the fall of Poland, he sent Germany thousands of tons of wheat, timber, and other raw materials as a sign of his good faith. He even had the NKVD turn over to the Gestapo German Communists who'd fled to Russia to escape Hitler.

Stalin couldn't believe his ears when told of Hitler's doublecross. For four hours after the attack, he forbid his armies to shoot back.

Hitler's invasion was the largest military operation in history. The Fuehrer sent 3.5 million men into battle on the first day.* These were supported by 600,000 vehicles, 3,400 tanks, 3,000 planes, and 7,200 cannon of various sizes.

The invaders came in three separate armies, each with its own special target. The central army under Field Marshal Fedor von Bock was the largest. Its mission was to smash through to Moscow, the Soviet capital and a vital railway and weapons-manufacturing center. The northern army under Field Marshal Wilhelm Ritter von Leeb aimed at Leningrad, Russia's second largest city and its best seaport. Field Marshal Gerd von Rundstedt's southern army was to occupy the Ukraine, Russia's breadbasket, where much of the nation's food is grown. Hitler believed the Communist state was so rotten that it would cave in within two months. It nearly did.

No nation ever suffered such losses at the beginning of a war as the Soviet Union. The Luftwaffe visited every airfield in western Russia during the war's first hours. Over two thousand planes were destroyed in the first two days of fighting. Luftwaffe chief Hermann Goering claimed to have knocked out over six thousand Russian planes within two weeks. Most were wrecked on the ground. The others, often outdated models flown by inexperienced pilots, were downed by Luftwaffe veterans.

Soviet ground forces were terribly mauled. The fast-moving panzers sliced into the country, often covering forty miles a day. Clouds of reddish dust hung in the

*A million of these were non-Germans sent by Rumania, Hungary, and Finland, all of which hated the Soviet Union and wanted Soviet territory.

western sky, marking their advance. The Soviets retreated in confusion or tried to hold out without air cover.

That's all Hitler's tank commanders needed. Two columns of tanks supported by self-propelled guns and infantry would move along parallel lines on either side of a Russian force. Suddenly one column would turn right, the other left, trapping the Russians in a "pocket" enclosing hundreds of square miles. The Germans then pressed inward from all sides, forcing the enemy to surrender or die. In several pockets, such as Minsk near the Polish border, 300,000 prisoners were taken in a few days.

Von Bock's central army became the star of the campaign. By mid-July, it had broken through the main Soviet defenses and was making a beeline for Moscow. The Soviet capital was Hitler's for the taking.

He would have taken Moscow had not success made him greedy. With Soviet resistance crumbling, he became like a sugar addict let loose in a candy factory. He wanted every-thing—now! But in trying to grab everything at once, he let go of the main prize, Moscow. That mistake may have cost him the war.

Things were going so well on the central front that he decided von Bock had more tanks than he needed. Most of his panzer divisions were sent to von Leeb and von Rund-stedt to speed up their advances. Von Bock, in the mean-time, was to carry on against Moscow with his remaining tanks and infantry.

Although opposed by the Wehrmacht high command, Hitler's decision seemed right at the time. Von Bock's drive slowed, but the others raced ahead with renewed strength. Panzers cut the Moscow–Leningrad railway, isolating Len-

Where the enemy passed, he left a desert. Russian villagers find relatives among the bodies of civilians murdered by German soldiers.

ingrad. Kiev and Kharkov fell, giving Hitler control of the Ukraine.

The world watched in stunned disbelief as Hitler went from one victory to another. By October 1, Russian losses came to 2.5 million men killed or captured, 22,000 guns, and 14,000 planes. Their tank forces, once larger than the whole world's combined, shrank from 15,000 to 700. It was a disaster.

The ex-corporal had shown them! Despite warnings from field marshals and generals, his "genius" and "intuition" had brought victory. A happy Fuehrer broadcast the good news to his people: "I declare . . . that the enemy in the East has been struck down and will never rise again." Once the panzers rejoined von Bock, Moscow would fall, and with it the Soviet Union. Great Britain, now without an ally, would have to beg him for peace.

That's not what happened. By slowing down von Bock for eight weeks (August–September 1941), Hitler gave the Russians time to rally their forces and prepare for a long war.

Stalin used the breathing space well. Although he'd blundered at the beginning, he never made another serious error for the rest of the war. He began to live up to his name, Stalin, "Man of Steel."

Orders flew from Stalin's office in the Kremlin, Moscow's ancient fortress with its red stone palaces and golden-domed churches. He was ruthless. One day he announced the Scorched Earth program. Russians must destroy anything that might be useful to the enemy if it fell into his hands. Penalty for disobedience: death.

Advancing Germans learned the meaning of Scorched

Hitler's Empire

U. S. S. R.

SWEDEN

NORWAY
Oslo •

FINLAND

• Leningrad

NORTH
SEA

ESTONIA

DENMARK

LATVIA

LITH.

★ Moscow

IRELAND

ENGLAND
London ★

NETH.

Berlin ★
BELG. GERMANY
Paris ★ LUX.

FRANCE

Prague ★
CZECH.

Vichy •

SWITZ.

Vienna ★
AUSTRIA

• Minsk

★ Warsaw
POLAND

Kiev •
Kharkov
•

Dnieper R.

Stalingrad

Volga

HUNGARY

Don R.

SPAIN

ITALY

★ Rome

YUGOSLAVIA

RUMANIA

BULGARIA

BLACK SEA

ALB.

GREECE

TURKEY

SYRIA

Sicily

MEDITERRANEAN SEA

LEBANON

IRA

TUNISIA

PALESTINE

TRANSJORDA

ALGERIA

El Alamein
• ★ Cairo

SAUDI
ARABIA

LIBYA

EGYPT

Area of Maxium Axis Rule (1941–42)
Neutral Nations

0   200   400 miles

Earth. Where once there had been farms, there was now wasteland. All around them, from horizon to horizon, were burning wheat fields. Peasants fled before the invaders, often burning their villages to deprive them of shelter. Wrecked bridges, caved-in tunnels, sunken river boats, and dynamited factories greeted them at every turn. The dam on the Dnieper River, largest on earth, was blown up by retreating Russians.

Stalin accepted no excuses for failure. On his orders Russian guns were turned on Russian fighting men. NKVD killing squads went to the front to weed out "traitors." Commanders who'd lost battles were declared traitors and shot as a warning to others. Thousands of common soldiers who'd run from the panzers faced firing squads. The purpose of this bloodbath was to make Russians more afraid of their own leaders than the enemy. It succeeded.

Hitler's gift of time also allowed Russia to mobilize her resources. Russia is a land blessed with natural wealth: iron ore, coal, oil, water, timber. Her people, though, are her most abundant resource. Russia in 1941 was a nation of 193 million, over 100 million more than Germany. She could take huge losses and still outnumber the enemy several times over.

The Russian soldier was affectionately known as Vanka, "Little Ivan." Germans learned to fear him more than any other enemy. Vanka was a rugged fellow, tough, stubborn, and brave. A peasant for the most part, he was a simple man used to long hours of heavy work in the open. Hardship didn't faze him. Where city-bred people would keel over from hunger and fatigue, Vanka kept fighting, ignoring discomfort. He knew how to bear pain, and seldom cried out when wounded.

Vanka might or might not like Stalin and the Communist dictatorship. But Russia—that was something else. He loved the Russian land. It wasn't merely earth or rock to him. It was holy, his "Mother Russia," his homeland. And for her he'd fight.

Moscow braced for the attack. Russia's largest city became an armed camp. Factory workers formed combat squads to patrol the streets in their off-hours. Machine-gun nests lined the rooftops. Every square and open space in the parks bristled with antiaircraft guns. The Moscow subway, one of the finest on earth, became a military railroad, ferrying troops to danger spots quickly and safely.

Each day a hundred thousand Muscovites marched into the countryside to work on the city's defenses. Working mostly with pick and shovel, they dug miles of trenches and tank traps, steep-sided ditches that no tank could escape once it fell over the edge. Most of the workers were women. They worked desperately, tirelessly, knowing the panzers were coming. "Those were terrible days," recalled a girl named Olga, whose three brothers were at the front.

> I was ordered, like most of the girls at the factory, to join the Labor Front. We were taken some kilometers out of Moscow. There was a large crowd of us, and we were told to dig trenches. We were all very calm, but dazed, and couldn't take it in. On the very first day we were machine-gunned by a Fritz who swooped right down. Eleven of the girls were killed and four wounded.

Resistance stiffened as von Bock's panzers renewed their drive. Now it was the Germans' turn to be amazed. Every trooper had stories about "mad Russians" sacrificing their lives to knock out one of the clanging monsters. A pilot crashed his burning fighter into a tank column. A soldier threw himself under a tank with a bunch of grenades, blowing himself up with it. Peasants made Molotov cocktails—named for Russia's foreign minister—gasoline-filled bottles with a rag wick stuck in the mouth. They'd leap aboard tanks, light the wick, and smash the bottle against a ventilator, killing themselves but frying the tank crew inside.

Von Bock's troops pushed ahead with every ounce of their strength. After months of steady fighting, they were tired. And frightened. As September gave way to October, the days grew shorter. Worse, each morning they noticed a white film on their weapons. Frost!

Everyone knew from history that a mighty army had once died in Russia. In 1812, the French emperor, Napoleon, had defeated every Russian commander except the one they called "General Winter." General Winter fought not with weapons, but with the forces of nature: cold, wind, fog, snow, sleet, ice. Napoleon's Grand Army hadn't died quickly or bravely in battle. It froze and starved in a whitened wasteland.

What if General Winter came before Germany won the war? Von Bock's troops wondered and worried.

General Winter arrived on November 19, and it was the worst winter in fifty years. The thermometer fell to 50° below zero in *daylight*. Winds from the North Pole howled at thirty miles an hour, making it feel like 80° below zero. Snow blanketed the ground, burying landmarks under mountainous drifts. Windblown snowflakes struck exposed skin like pebbles from slingshots.

General Winter played the devil with Hitler's armies. *Der Fuehrer*, expecting an easy victory, had refused to winterize army equipment. As a result, machines of all kinds broke down in the subzero temperatures. The water in locomotive boilers turned to blocks of ice. Truck engines froze and died. Tanks became helpless when telescopic gunsights froze. In order to start tank engines, fires had to be kept burning beneath them. Gasoline froze and burst fuel lines. Lubricating oil in cannon and small arms thickened into black, gooey globs.

The German soldier suffered worst, facing General Winter in a summer uniform and whatever clothing he could steal from Russian villagers. The "Winter Fritz" wrapped his head in women's handkerchiefs, wore woolen dresses, and was glad to get a raggedy cloth coat. His feet froze in boots that fit exactly, making it impossible to wear more than one pair of socks. The flesh of gloveless hands peeled off in strips on ice-cold gun barrels and triggers. Unwashed men stank and crawled with lice, gray crablike creatures that drove them crazy with itching.

German field hospitals filled to overflowing with cases of pneumonia, snow-blindness, and frostbite. The only treatment for frost-bitten limbs was amputation, although medicines and painkillers were in short supply. Doctors did the best they could, but patients continued to die of shock and infection.

Marching troops passed low, white mounds: their comrades. Wounded men died where they fell, cemented to the ground by their own frozen blood. Exhausted men sat in the snow to rest, fell asleep, and never awoke. Radio Moscow broadcast the same message around the clock: "Every

seven seconds a German dies in Russia. *Tick, tick, tick,
BONG!"* Russia was hell frozen over.

Russian people, however, understand winter and how to
prepare for it. Soviet troops wore fur jackets, fur gloves, and
fur hats with ear flaps. Best of all were their *valenki*, soft
felt boots roomy enough for two pairs of woolen socks.

Russian snipers dressed for their deadly work. Each man
had a long white cape lined with fur. He'd lie in a snowfield,
motionless for hours, waiting. The black uniforms of the
Weapons SS made good targets against the snow. *Bang!* A
shot from nowhere, and another Nazi fell.

German generals begged for permission to pull back to
defensive positions and wait out the winter. But Hitler,
seated in his heated headquarters, wouldn't hear of calling
off the drive. "No withdrawal!" he'd yell at the top of his
voice. "Not a single yard of retreat!" He wanted Moscow
and would have it at any cost.

Von Bock's army inched forward. Losses skyrocketed, but
each day brought it closer to its objective. By December 4,
patrols broke into the city's southern outskirts. Off in the
distance, glinting in the pale sunlight, they glimpsed the
golden domes of the Kremlin. Then they died in their
tracks.

The next week changed the course of the Second World
War. Early in October, the spy Richard Sorge made Stalin
a gift of two million trained soldiers. Russia had a vast army
in Siberia to keep watch on the Japanese, who'd been fighting in China for ten years. There had been border clashes,
and Stalin feared a Japanese invasion if he moved the Siberian army to Moscow's defense.

As the panzers advanced, Sorge learned a secret. Japan's

war lords had decided against invading Russia in favor of
challenging Great Britain and the United States in the Pacific. A carrier task force was already at sea. Its target: Pearl
Harbor in the Hawaiian Islands. Date of attack: Sunday,
December 7, 1941.

This time Stalin believed his spy. Secretly most of the
Siberian army moved west along the Trans-Siberian Railroad. Its troops were unlike any seen by the Germans. Asiat-
ics, they were short, wiry men with slanted eyes, high
cheekbones, and straight black hair. Most spoke little Russian, but Kalmuk, the language of Mongolia and the plains
of Central Asia. Their ancestors had ridden with Genghis
Khan, "Conqueror of the World," and they were the fiercest
warriors in the Red Army.

The Siberians were massing in and around Moscow when
von Bock's patrols saw the Kremlin. On December 6 they
slammed into the invaders like a runaway express train. The
Germans, already pushed to their limits by cold and combat,
fell back. Japanese planes bombed Pearl Harbor the next
day.

Der Fuehrer despised the United States. "Americans,"
he'd say, "have the brains of a hen." He thought them weak
and cowardly, a "racially corrupt" nation whose blood had
been poisoned by Jews and Blacks. His race hatred so blinded
him to America's strengths that he joined Japan in its war,
December 11, 1941.

Once the United States entered the war, it pledged to
fight until both Hitler and Japan were defeated. President
Franklin D. Roosevelt declared America the "Arsenal of
Democracy." The wheels of American industry began to
turn faster, producing a flood of war materials for its British

and Soviet allies. Slowly but surely *der Fuehrer* was digging
the Third Reich's grave.

During the winter of 1941, Vanka saw the face of Hitlerism
in all its ugliness. It was one thing to fight Germans with
weapons, man to man. Soldiers are supposed to kill and be
killed for their countries. But prisoners of war and civilians?
Civilized nations had always tried to spare them.

The Germans took their lead from their Fuehrer, who
took pride in being a barbarian. Russian prisoners were
deliberately mistreated. Men captured in the great pockets
were shot immediately or sent to die of starvation, disease,
and cold. Tens of thousands of prisoners were gathered in
barren snowfields, penned in with barbed wire, and then
robbed of their warm clothing. Germans told in letters home
of how men howled like tortured beasts until they froze.
Others were sheltered in filthy barns, but not fed. Russian
prisoners became so desperate that they sometimes became
cannibals to save their lives. Hermann Goering thought this
a big joke; he laughed when told how starving Russians ate
one of their German guards. About 3.5 million Soviet
war prisoners were murdered during the Second World
War.

In retaking their towns after Moscow, Vanka and his
tovarish, his comrades, got firsthand experience of the "Master Race." Everywhere the Germans destroyed what they
couldn't use or carry away. Everywhere civilians—the elderly, women, children—were murdered and tortured. In-
fants were held by their feet and their heads smashed against
walls. When Mother Russia was finally liberated, she'd lost
1,700 cities and 70,000 villages—all completely destroyed;

War without mercy. This photograph, taken from a captured German soldier, shows SS field police executing Russian prisoners. First the victims were forced to dig their own graves, then they were tumbled in.

no fewer than 20 million of her people died, the highest
loss for any nation in any war.

Hatred welled up in the people. Meeting on the street,
ordinary citizens, who'd never dreamed of hurting another
person, exchanged the greeting, "Comrade, have you killed
your German today?" Stalin, the tyrant, nevertheless knew
what was in people's hearts. In one speech he said:

> The German invaders want a war of extermination
> against the peoples of the Soviet Union. Very well
> then! If they want a war of extermination they shall
> have it! Our task now . . . will be to destroy every
> German, to the very last man, who has come to
> occupy our country. No mercy to the German in-
> vaders! Death to the German invaders!

The Russians began guerrilla warfare. Hitler's soldiers
found themselves fighting the Red Army at the front and
an enraged people behind the lines. Peasants took to the
forests, where they were trained and armed by special units
of the Red Army. Many others spied on the Germans,
reporting their every activity to the guerrillas.

Night belonged to the guerrillas. Parties of five, ten, or
fifty, depending upon the mission, left the forests under
cover of darkness. Everything German was fair game. Troop
trains were derailed, truck convoys ambushed, and supply
depots blown up.

No German or German supporter felt safe anywhere,
even in bed. Pretty young girls became assassins, like the
teenager who flirted with a German officer and then put a
bomb under his bed. German patrols were cut off and outposts raided. Enemy soldiers were seldom allowed to sur-

render. Guerrillas had to travel lightly and fast, too fast to worry about prisoners. SS men were killed on sight. They were shot or made to die slowly in payment for the crimes of the SS.

Russian traitors received no mercy. Guerrillas would sneak into a village at night, drag a traitor from bed, and execute him in front of the whole community. They were lucky. The unlucky ones were turned over to the peasant women to be beaten to death with rakes and hoes.

Guerrilla warfare in Russia was a savage, no-holds-barred struggle. Hitler, who'd provoked it, ordered towns destroyed in reprisal for giving guerrillas so much as a drink of water. Hostages were taken and slaughtered if their families didn't betray guerrilla hideouts. Hitler called guerrillas "terrorists"; they saw themselves as patriots fighting for their homes and to avenge murdered innocents.

The winter of 1941 was hardest on the three million citizens of Leningrad. The story of Leningrad, like that of London, is one of a people's courage and refusal to bow to a vicious enemy. It is a story that is at once horrible and inspiring.

Leningrad—Lenin City—is named for the father of the Russian Revolution. It was there, in Russia's old capital,* that V. I. Lenin first led the Communists in overthrowing the czar's government in 1917–1918. Lying at the eastern end of the Gulf of Finland, Leningrad is a city of wide avenues, magnificent palaces, and museums filled with art treasures. Like Venice in Italy, it has a network of canals spanned by six hundred bridges. Leningrad's shipyards and

* St. Petersburg, renamed Leningrad in 1924.

factories were (and are) among the largest in the Soviet Union. One of its offshore islands is the Soviet "Pearl Harbor," home port of its largest warships.

News that Field Marshal von Leeb's northern army was on the move came as a thunderbolt. Troops were rushed to Leningrad and civilians put to work on the defenses, which soon outgrew even Moscow's. Trenches and tank traps covered hundreds of square miles. Every way into the city was blocked by thickets of barbed wire laced with mines and machine-gun nests.

These defenses, however, were only the city's outer shell. Leningraders vowed to make the German army break its teeth on their city. The Nazis would have to fight for every inch of ground. Barricades of concrete reinforced with lengths of railroad track were set up at street intersections. Concrete pillboxes nested inside houses in such a way that the defenders could keep fighting even if the building collapsed on top of them. Leningrad had no subway, but its network of deep sewers was useful in moving supplies and men in safety underground.

One more thing: All bridges, power plants, docks, shops, warehouses, museums, factories, and government buildings were mined, along with thousands of ordinary houses. The moment the Germans seemed to be winning, Leningrad would have been blown up. That was Stalin's decision, and Leningraders supported it. Their choice was simple: die bravely amid the ruins of their city, or live under the whips of Hitler's slave drivers.

On September 9, 1941, von Leeb's panzers cut the rail lines linking Leningrad to the rest of Russia. Now its only contact with the outside world was by boat across Lake

Lagoda to the north, and this route was constantly patrolled by the Luftwaffe. The alarm sounded: "The enemy is at the gates."

Hitler made it clear that he meant to destroy Leningrad and its people. He issued written orders to his generals that the city mustn't be allowed to surrender, but levelled to the ground and everyone killed. To do this, he ordered the largest guns in Europe aimed at the city. These "railroad guns" were so large that each needed its own train to move it and its ammunition; each shell was taller than a man and weighed a thousand pounds.

Shells and bombs rained on Leningrad. A sound like an enormous bedsheet tearing overhead was followed by an explosion that shook the earth and blew out windows. The enemy guns were answered by Red Army batteries and by the warships anchored offshore. People got used to the noise and, in time, didn't take cover unless a shell seemed about to land nearby.

Leningrad's children saw death daily. You seldom went into the streets without passing mangled bodies and pools of blood. Children themselves were special targets. German planes delivered Christmas "presents" designed to kill. They dropped booby traps disguised as toys, dolls, fountain pens, and chocolate bars. The instant you touched a booby trap, it exploded.

Leningrad's deadliest enemies were cold and hunger, and they worked silently. General Winter held the city in his icy grip. Pipes froze and burst, leaving homes without water for toilets and washing; water for cooking had to be carried in pails from the Neva River, which flows through the city. But even with water, people seldom washed. Fuel was scarce and had to be used to run the defense factories. None could be spared for heating water or lighting—or fire engines. Firemen had to let whole blocks of apartment houses burn. Nobody minded, except the tenants; people came from miles around to warm themselves near the flames.

People burned whatever they could to heat their homes. Books and furniture went into the stoves. Ten thousand wooden buildings were torn down for firewood. Still Leningraders slept in overcoats, hats, and boots. Their darkened city smelled of dirt, charred wood, and wet stone. "Even the tears froze within the people of Leningrad," a survivor recalled.

Undernourished people easily took sick in the cold. Food had been rationed early in the siege, and everyone was given a ration card once a month. The card entitled you to a certain amount of food, depending on your age and job. Soldiers and factory workers received the most; housewives, the elderly, and children the least, because they weren't necessary for the city's defense.

Food was scarce even with rationing. What little there was had to be stretched to go a long way. Thus bread bakers added plaster and fine sawdust to flour. The two thousand tons of sheep guts found in a slaughterhouse were made into jelly; the slimy mass looked awful and tasted worse, but hungry people gulped it down.

Leningraders filled their bellies in any way they could. Women stopped trying to make themselves look pretty; instead lipsticks, face powder, and hair oil were eaten. People chewed plaster and gnawed the bark off trees. They tore wallpaper off walls and ate the dried paste; furniture was smashed to get at the glue. Leather belts and briefcases went into the cooking pot. Dogs and cats disappeared. Bats and mice were hardly seen anymore.

It was a losing battle for many. People appeared every day in the snow-covered streets pulling children's sleds. The sleds were painted bright yellow or red, and each had a body that family members were taking to a cemetery for burial. Often the person pulling the sled died before reaching his destination. Cold and starvation claimed the lives of 4,000–6,000 Leningraders a day during the Starvation Winter of 1941; on certain days as many as 10,000 died.

Starvation weakened people's bodies, but not their determination to resist to the end. Factory workers stayed at their machines during the heaviest shellings. Sometimes shells plunged through a roof, exploding in the midst of a group of workers. The survivors tended their machines, while clean-up squads removed bodies and cleared rubble. Leningraders had seen so much, suffered so terribly, that they were beyond fear.

Posters reminded them about what they were fighting for. Said one, "If today he does not fight bravely in defense of the city, then tomorrow he will lose his honor and freedom, his native home, and become a German slave."

Schools kept their doors open whenever possible. Half-starved children left home before dawn and walked through shell-torn streets to get to school on time. School became more than a place of learning during the siege. It meant shared feelings and the moral support of people one's own age. School was a way of forgetting for a few hours the hunger, cold, and grief.

A war diary was kept by the pupils of one school, boys and girls aged ten to sixteen. It is called *Our Famine Scrapbook* and contains essays written during the siege. From it we learn how it felt to hold classes in bomb shelters, and to see a teacher killed by a shell in the schoolyard. Luba Tereshchnekova, a girl of sixteen, described school life during the Starvation Winter:

> In January and February [1942] terrible frost also joined in the blockade and lent Hitler a hand. (It was never less than thirty degrees below zero!) Our classes continued on the "Round the Stove" principle. But there were no reserved seats, and if you wanted a seat near the stove or under the stove pipe, you had to come early. The place facing the stove door was reserved for the teacher. You sat down and were suddenly seized by a wonderful feeling of well-being: the warmth penetrated through your skin, right into your bones; it made you all weak and languid; you just wanted to think of nothing, only to slumber and drink in the warmth. It was agony to stand up and go to the blackboard. . . . At the blackboard it was so cold and dark, and your hand, imprisoned in its heavy glove, went all numb and rigid and refused to obey. The chalk kept falling out of your hand, and the lines were all crooked. . . . By the time we reached the third lesson there was no more fuel left. The stove went cold and a horrid icy draught started blowing down the pipe. It became terribly cold. It was then that Vasya Pugin, with a puckish look on his face, could be seen slinking out and bringing in a few logs from Anna Ivanovna's emergency reserve; and a few minutes later, we could again hear the magic crackling of wood inside the stove. . . . During the break nobody would jump

up because nobody had any desire to go into the icy
corridors.

People became desperate as the siege dragged on month
after month. Some stole food or killed for it. An old woman
walking home with a few ounces of sawdust-and-flour bread
after waiting hours outside a bakery might be hit over the
head; men were stabbed for a morsel of stringy horsemeat.
Stealing a ration card was the same as murder, for the victim
had to wait until next month for a replacement.

Leningrad policemen made short work of "food criminals." Patrols stopped suspicious persons and, if they had
stolen ration cards or more food than usual, shot them on
the spot. No arrest. No trial. Executions took place in the
streets every day and became a common sight.

Leningrad's only hope lay in Lake Lagoda, the largest
lake in Europe. In November 1941, at the very moment
Hitler's troops were freezing outside Moscow, the surface
of Lake Lagoda became a foot-thick sheet of ice. From then
until the thaw next April, that sheet of ice became the city's
Road of Life.

Each day truck convoys loaded with food sped along the
Road of Life at forty miles an hour. First-aid stations, repair
shops, and traffic control points sprang up on the ice to
keep them moving. Antiaircraft guns and fighter planes
guarded the route.

Try as they might, the Germans couldn't close the Road
of Life. Railroad guns and Stukas wrecked hundreds of
trucks, but the traffic flow continued. Nature repaired any
damage caused by explosives. Holes blasted in the roadway
were sealed with new ice within hours.

Although it was never enough, and people still died by the thousands, trucked-in food saved Leningrad. People welcomed truck drivers as heroes. One day an old *babushka*, a grandma, stood in line at a bakery. When given her ration, a small loaf of coarse black bread, she stared at it a moment. "It is Lagoda bread. It is holy bread," she said for all to hear. Then she crossed herself and kissed it.

Life became easier after the Starvation Winter. Eventually the Red Army forced a corridor through the German lines and kept it open despite heavy losses. Yet the siege continued until January 1944.

Never in history had so large a city withstood a 900-day siege. As many as 1.5 million Leningraders died during the siege, more than have ever died in any other modern city. Leningraders lost much, but in the end they still had their honor and self-respect. For they, like the Londoners, had proven that they could take the worst Hitler could hand out and come back fighting.

In Berlin, meanwhile, Adolf Hitler read reports from the front. True, 1941 had brought setbacks. His armies had fallen back two hundred miles from Moscow before setting up strong defense lines; at last warm clothing was arriving from the Reich. Leningrad still held out. Losses had been heavy: 750,000 Germans killed, wounded, and missing after five months of fighting.

Yet there was a bright side. *Der Fuehrer* always saw the bright side of things, even if others saw only gloom. His forces still held most of European Russia. His troops were tough and battle-hardened. German industry could replace lost machines and build new, improved models.

As winter gave way to spring, Hitler planned a new campaign. He promised himself that 1942 would be his year, the year he destroyed the Soviet Union.

Hitler decided that the road to victory lay in the south, along the banks of the Volga River. The Volga, a mile wide in places, is the connecting link between the Soviet oil fields near Turkey and the northern industrial cities. Cutting the Volga would make Stalin's war machine grind to a halt for lack of fuel. It would also allow the panzers to make a wide sweep northward, taking Moscow from the east.

The key to the southern Volga was Stalin City—Stalingrad.* Sprawling for thirty-five miles along the west bank of the Volga, this city of a half million was a real prize. In addition to its strategic location, Stalingrad was a major producer of farm machinery, tanks, and guns; oil refineries, warehouses, and shipyards crowded its waterfront.

Not everyone shared Hitler's enthusiasm for Stalingrad. Several high-ranking officers warned against going deeper into Russia. Germany was fighting the three most powerful nations on earth and could not afford more heavy losses. For them the lesson of the past winter was clear: Germany simply lacked the strength or the manpower to conquer Russia.

Field Marshals von Rundstedt and von Leeb urged Hitler to forget about Stalingrad. He should, indeed, pull back his armies further, have them dig in, and hold on to whatever they could. Loyal Nazis, they were also able soldiers with sense enough to quit while they were ahead.

Not their Fuehrer. When Hitler heard their advice, he stamped his feet in anger. "Idiots!" he yelled. He refused

*It was renamed Volgograd after the dictator's death in 1953.

to hear such "nonsense" and dismissed everyone who questioned his plan. He'd shown them before and he would show them again. His stubbornness and vanity triggered the Battle of Stalingrad, the greatest land battle of the Second World War.

Hitler gave the Sixth Army the "honor" of taking Stalingrad. The Sixth Army under General Friedrich von Paulus had made a fine record earlier in the war. Von Paulus, a tall, handsome man of fifty-two, was an experienced soldier who knew a bad plan when he saw it. And Hitler's plan was awful. Worse, he'd lost faith in the Fuehrer. "Hitler was a maniac," he told a friend after the war. "I knew that from the first." Yet he clicked his heels, snapped a *Heil Hitler!* salute, and obeyed orders.

As a professional soldier, von Paulus believed it his duty to obey Germany's leader, whoever he might be. To men like him, disobedience was worse than fighting a battle he knew he couldn't win. Orders, right or wrong, were sacred in his eyes. That was sad; for only when it was too late, when the Sixth Army was destroyed, did he realize his mistake. Then he understood that his duty as a man outweighed his oath to a "maniac" in Berlin.

The men of the Sixth Army, however, trusted their Fuehrer when they set off for Stalingrad on June 22, 1942, the first anniversary of Operation Barbarossa. The Sixth Army advanced in huge hollow squares with trucks, troop carriers, and artillery enclosed in a frame of tanks. It moved under a canopy of fighter planes and a dust cloud that rose thousands of feet into the blue sky. The air was thick with dust, gunsmoke, and the smoke of burning villages.

The panzers seemed irresistible, like an elephant herd

trampling everything in its path. Villages were abandoned, and peasants, bowed under bundles of their possessions, trekked eastward. Soviet forces retreated, pausing only to fight rearguard actions. Mostly, though, resistance was so slight that tank crews had time to swim in rivers along the way. The grimy troops stripped naked and, laughing, splashed in the warm water.

The water felt good, but the thought of victory felt best. Russia's end was near, and soon the Sixth Army would be going home to a hero's welcome. "We shall soon see each other," a soldier wrote his wife on August 7. "All of us feel that the end, victory, is near." A few days later, scouts seized the Kalach railroad bridge over the Don River, the last natural barrier before Stalingrad.

Forty miles to the east, Stalingrad sweltered in the heat of the southern steppes. The steppes are a vast tableland stretching into Asia, barren except for short grass. The climate of the steppes is one of extremes. Summer temperatures reach 110° and a blowtorch of a wind turns the grass brown. Dust particles cling to sweaty skin and crackle between the teeth. Winters are bone-chilling.

Ignoring the heat, every able-bodied Stalingrader turned out to dig tank traps on the steppe west of the city. Work was going well when von Paulus gave them a taste of what was coming.

On the afternoon of August 23, sirens wailed in Stalingrad. Loudspeakers in the streets boomed out a recorded message: "Attention. Attention. Citizens, we have an air raid! We have an air raid!" Cars screeched to a halt. Buses let off passengers who, stopping for a moment, heard the droning from the west.

Six hundred Nazi planes soared overhead in V-formations. All day and far into the night they unloaded their bombs. Because of the dry heat, thousands of wooden buildings caught fire at once. Within minutes Stalingrad was a sea of fire; only larger buildings of steel and concrete survived. Oil tanks on the shore flamed, burst, and poured their contents into the Volga. The current carried great patches of burning oil downstream so that the river itself seemed on fire. Over forty thousand people died in this one raid.

This tragedy convinced the government that Stalingrad was no place for civilians. During the following days, a two-way traffic flowed across the Volga. Civilians crossing to safety in the east passed boatloads of Red Army men heading for their city. The boats, many with passengers jammed so tightly they couldn't move, attracted enemy fighters. The Germans swooped down for the kill with screeching sirens and chattering machine guns. When they passed, patches of red spread out from the broken boats. The riverbanks became choked with bodies that bloated and stank in the heat.

The Russian commander in Stalingrad was forty-two-year-old General Vasili I. Chuikov, a Red Army veteran with a deeply lined face and a sparkling smile: all his teeth had gold crowns that sparkled in the sunlight. Chuikov's job was to hold Stalingrad until the Soviet high command worked out a plan to deal with the invaders. Chuikov knew that the Sixth Army outnumbered his own Sixty-second Army. Yet he had two weapons that weighed heavily in his favor: his men's courage and Stalingrad itself. He would fight at close quarters, never giving the enemy time to rest or regroup. And he'd fight for *everything*, forcing von Paulus to pay in blood for the slightest gain.

Of course, Stalingrad would be totally destroyed during the fighting. Good. For the ruins would provide Chuikov's men with cover and become a graveyard for the Nazis. The Russians had stopped running and would defend their city to the end.

The Germans had seen plenty of fighting, but nothing to match Stalingrad. Their mood quickly changed from happiness to surprise—to terror. Soldiers scribbled notes in diaries calling Stalingrad's defenders "fanatics," "wild beasts," "devils." "The Russians are not men," one wrote, "but some kind of cast-iron creatures; they never get tired and are not afraid of fire." The Russians took this diary and many others from the bodies of fallen Germans.

The invaders met men like Mikhail Panikako, a member of a machine-gun team detailed to hold off tanks advancing toward a factory. Mikhail's ammunition ran out and, grabbing two Molotov cocktails, he lit the fuse of the first one. As he drew back his arm to throw it, a bullet hit the bottle and ignited the gasoline, turning him into a human torch. Without a word or cry of pain, Mikhail ran forward with the other bottle and threw himself under the tank, killing himself and the tank's five-man crew.

The Nazis might also meet women fighters at Stalingrad. Russia proved during the Second World War that women could fight as well as men in the front lines. At its peak strength, the Red Army had one million female scouts, truck drivers, military police, traffic controllers, artillery gunners, machine gunners, and tank crews. Squads of female soldiers toted rifles and tossed hand grenades.

The Russians were especially proud of their pilots of the 596th Fighter Wing. This all-woman outfit saw action over Stalingrad and in many other air battles. Some 596th pilots chalked up records that would have earned medals in any air force. Valerie Khomyakova was the first woman to shoot down an enemy plane at night. The Germans called her the Flying Witch, because she'd take any risk to get a shot at them. Marina Chechneva made 810 combat flights, more than any member of the United States Army Air Forces during the war. One of her friends, a slim, blond twenty-year-old, shot down a Nazi ace over Stalingrad. When told that he'd fallen to a woman, he sputtered with rage and refused to believe the story. Only later, when he met her and heard her account, did he fall into red-faced silence.

In the meantime, the Battle of Stalingrad raged on the ground. It was no blitzkrieg, but a fierce slugging match. By the end of September 1942, von Paulus had taken the center of the city, but at tremendous cost. Chuikov fought him street by street, house by house, room by room from basement to rooftop. When streets were flattened, he fought him for possession of the ruins.

Chuikov had filled Stalingrad with strongpoints, which the Nazis had to capture before moving forward. Artillery hammered buildings into rubble, then churned up the rubble. Panzers then rumbled down the streets, searching for Russian strongpoints. They'd work over a building with pointblank cannon fire, only to run into a hail of grenades and antitank rifles that fired armor-piercing bullets. The streets, choked with wreckage from collapsed buildings, prevented the tanks from maneuvering. If a tank was disabled, others had to push it aside or back away at full speed.

When German assault teams rushed a building, they found themselves in a hide-and-seek fight for their lives. The Russians seemed to grow out of the ground of Stalingrad. For every man killed, there was always another to take his place. Chuikov's men knocked communicating holes through the attics and basements of adjoining buildings, enabling them to bring up reinforcements without being spotted by cruising tanks.

A battle for a single house might seesaw back and forth for three weeks without letup. As the Russians abandoned a floor, they sowed boobytraps in every nook and cranny. A wrong move would cost a German an arm, a leg, his eyes, his life.

The Germans would finally clear a building to the roof, only to find that Red Army men had reoccupied the lower floors. A narrow hallway became a no-man's-land with soldiers shooting and tossing grenades from either side. Russians were seen to catch grenades and throw them back. This was dangerous work, for if you missed your timing, the grenade exploded in your face.

Germans holed up in cellars found that the Russians had a nasty habit. While comrades in a nearby house opened fire to cover the sounds, they'd tunnel from the house next door and set a mine, say fifty sticks of dynamite.

Captain Ignacy Changar was an expert mine-layer. He once lit a fuse and shouted for his men to run for their lives. Moments later the building, a large apartment house, rose into the air amid a ball of fire. When the dust settled, Changar counted 180 German bodies.

Constant fighting with little food and less sleep wore down the German soldiers. Many became shell-shocked, shaking

The factories of Stalingrad, one of the Soviet Union's major industrial cities, burn behind a bombed-out wasteland.

and crying uncontrollably. "My God, have you forsaken us?" Lieutenant Weiner of the 24th Panzer Division wrote in his diary. He continued:

> We have fought during fifteen days for a single house, with mortars, grenades, machine guns, and bayonets. Already by the third day fifty-four German corpses are strewn in the cellars, on the landings, and the staircases. The front is a corridor between burned-out rooms; it is the thin ceiling between two floors. Help comes from neighboring houses by fire escapes and chimneys. There is a ceaseless struggle from noon to night. From story to story, faces black with sweat, we bombard each other with grenades in the middle of explosions, clouds of dust and smoke, heaps of mortar, floods of blood, fragments of furniture and human bodies. Ask any soldier what half an hour of hand-to-hand struggle means in such a fight. And imagine Stalingrad; eighty days and eighty nights of hand-to-hand struggles. The street is no longer measured by meters but by corpses. . . .
>
> Stalingrad is no longer a town. . . . it is an enormous cloud of burning, blinding smoke; it is a vast furnace lit by the reflection of the flames.

Stalingrad never slept. The skeletons of broken buildings cast eerie shadows in the moonlight. Watchful eyes, snipers' eyes, peered from the shadows. The slightest movement on the enemy side drew their attention. The hunt was on, although the would-be victim didn't know it until too late.

Night or day, snipers took a heavy toll at Stalingrad. Snipers had high-powered rifles with telescopic sights. They could be anywhere: on rooftops, under rubble, or peering through a tiny crack in a brick wall. Calm, patient people, they'd sit still for hours, barely moving a muscle, to get in the one shot that killed.

Germans had a healthy respect for Russian snipers. At Stalingrad women joined men in the special sniper squads. Among them was Tania Chernova, a twenty-year-old blonde who forgot her dreams of becoming a doctor when Barbarossa began. Tania joined the army and found that she was a natural with a rifle. She so hated the Germans that she could never think of them as people, but only as "sticks." Before a wound ended her sniping career, Tania "broke" forty sticks at Stalingrad.

The Sixth Army pushed ahead. By November 1942, von Paulus could radio the Fuehrer that he held nearly all of Stalingrad. The city's defenders were now penned into three small pockets along the Volga. Yet, despite furious attacks, they hung on, refusing to be driven into the river.

Back at headquarters, von Paulus' fellow officers were worried. They remembered the last November, when General Winter suddenly turned the Moscow front into a frozen hell. Winter gear was being sent, but transportation foul-ups had stalled hundreds of supply trains in out-of-the-way railroad stations in Poland. Worse, they had reports of enemy activity north and south of Stalingrad, where the German lines were weakest. A Soviet counterattack there might mean disaster. The high command shuddered at the thought of the Sixth Army, 280,000 men, trapped during the winter in a ruined city without winter clothing.

Hitler wouldn't listen to such "foolishness." He and Stalin

were no longer fighting over a city, but for their pride. These dictators, although very powerful men, were also very small men. By boasting of their greatness, they dared not admit failure. Retreat would have been an admission of defeat, a shaming of themselves in their own eyes and in the eyes of the world. And so the Battle of Stalingrad had to be fought to the finish, no matter how many lives were lost.

Most of those lives would be German. The Russians had used the time Chuikov's men bought for them to plan and gather their forces for an enormous counterattack. At dawn, November 19, 1942, they were ready.

A million fresh troops waited at their jump-off points. Artillery stood wheel to wheel in rows, one row behind the other, ten and twenty deep. Thousands of trucks were parked with their *Katyushkas*. *Katyushka*, or Little Kate, was a rocket launcher that looked like rows of organ pipes mounted on a flatbed truck. Each launcher sent off sixteen rockets at once, more firepower than a destroyer's.

It was still dark when Chuikov's men heard distant rumbling. Putting their heads out of their dugouts, they grinned and passed the word, *"Nachalos!"*—"It has started!"

Never in this war had the Germans been under such a bombardment. The Russian big guns spoke, and the ground shook as in an earthquake. The sound of individual guns became lost in a steady, earsplitting roar. Soldiers standing nearby saw guns belch smoke rings and felt the vibrations in their guts.

Minutes passed, then Little Kate lent her voice to the din. Streaks of orange-red stabbed the gray dawn as rockets sprang from their launch tubes. All you could hear was a steady BAROOM mingled with a constant WHOOSH-WHOOSH-WHOOSH.

The effect was shattering. Clusters of shells dropped into the German lines. Gun batteries vanished into smoking shell holes. Vehicles—tanks, trucks, staff cars, troop carriers, gasoline tankers—became masses of blackened junk. *Katyushkas*, exploding together by the thousands at ground level, sent steel splinters zinging through the air.

As the bombardment lifted, dazed Germans heard a dreaded sound. Out of the mist rose the clatter of T-34 tanks mingled with the battle cry of masses of foot soldiers. Thirty-four tons of pure trouble, the new tank was heavier, faster, and easier to handle than anything in the Nazi arsenal. Antitank shells bounced off its armor-plated sides; only direct hits with the largest artillery shells could stop a T-34.

The Russians moved crosscountry, north and south of Stalingrad, then turned inward, meeting like the jaws of an immense bear trap. They took the bridge at Kalach, over which every bean and bullet used by the Sixth Army passed. Within three days, the Sixth Army was trapped in the ruined city.

Yet all was not lost. The Sixth Army was ringed by a million Russians, but the ring was still thin. Now was the time to act, before the enemy widened his front and dug in. If von Paulus concentrated his forces at one point in the ring, he'd surely burst through the trap.

Unfortunately, permission for a breakout had to come from Hitler personally. The very idea of retreat threw *der Fuehrer* into a temper tantrum. He raged. He cursed. He banged his fists on his map table. "I won't leave the Volga!" he screamed. He radioed orders that the Sixth Army must hold Stalingrad unto death.

All efforts to free the Sixth Army failed. Each time relieving forces drew near, they ran into a wall of *Katyushkas* and T-34s. Attempts at resupplying von Paulus by air failed. Fog and Soviet fighters prevented all but a few transports from getting through. Often it broke the troops' hearts to see parachuted supplies drift over the Russian lines.

Slowly the Sixth Army was squeezed into an ever-shrinking pocket. By December 1942, General Winter returned with snow and subzero temperatures. Now the Nazis began to understand what Leningraders had suffered the previous winter.

Europe's conquerors lived in crowded cellars with slime oozing down the walls. Their bellies swollen with hunger, they shivered in the darkness. Medical supplies ran out, forcing doctors to operate without painkillers. Simple scratches attracted lice, lice brought germs, and wounds that could have been treated with a few daubs of iodine became deadly.

Men recorded their sufferings in diaries. Wrote one:

> *Dec. 7.* No change. Oh God, help me to return safe and sound! My poor wife, my dear father and mother! How hard it is for them now. God Almighty, put an end to this torture! Give us peace again. . . .
>
> *Dec. 12.* Still in Stalingrad. . . . I am frightfully hungry. If things eased up a bit. Only not get sick or be wounded. God in Heaven, protect me.

The diary ends here.

The writer's Fuehrer didn't care about his suffering. Not once during the agony of the Sixth Army did Hitler show sympathy for the men who served him so loyally. When told of the daily losses, he replied, "But that's what the young men are there for!" They were in Stalingrad to win or to die for him.

Von Paulus' officers pleaded with him to try a breakout while part of the army might still be saved. He refused. He had a direct Fuehrer order which he must obey. The slaughter continued.

On January 30, 1943, the tenth anniversary of Hitler's taking power, von Paulus sent his last message. The Sixth Army was doomed. If he didn't surrender immediately, thousands would die needlessly.

Hitler radioed, "A German army does not surrender." He also promoted von Paulus to field marshal. But since no German field marshal had ever been taken alive, the Fuehrer was inviting him to earn his promotion by committing suicide.

At last something clicked in von Paulus' brain. Suddenly he realized the full measure of Hitler's selfishness. Von Paulus believed in the strict code of honor of the German army. For most officers honor meant fighting to the end; suicide was preferable to capture or a "dishonorable" escape. But to Hitler "loyalty," "honor," and "duty" were only words he used to control others, not things he believed in himself. The next day, Field Marshal Friedrich von Paulus surrendered the remnants of the Sixth Army.

For the first time in the Second World War, a high-ranking officer had disobeyed a direct order from his Fuehrer. Von Paulus felt sad, but relieved; for in disobeying, he'd regained his dignity as a man.

Hitler flew into a rage when news of the surrender reached his headquarters. Here, he shouted, the thick veins standing out in his neck, he'd "generously" promoted von Paulus to the highest honor, only to be "ungratefully" betrayed. True, the field marshal had been under terrific strain, but, said

Hitler, "A pistol makes it all easy. How cowardly can you be, to be afraid of something like that?"

Von Paulus' disobedience came too late for the Sixth Army. Its losses were huge: 61,000 vehicles, 8,000 guns, 1,550 tanks, 235 ammunition dumps. Of the 280,000 men encircled in November, 91,000 were around to surrender in January. These were marched across the snow-covered steppes to prison camps in distant Siberia; only 6,000 of these lived to see their homes again. The rest died of beatings, starvation, and overwork during the years of captivity that followed. The last Stalingrad captive returned in 1955, ten years after the war. Even today, no one outside the Soviet government knows how many Russians died in the Battle of Stalingrad.

Stalingrad convinced Hitler that professional soldiers were fools and weaklings. Since they couldn't be trusted, he decided that he must direct everything personally. From then on, he meddled in every plan, dismissing brilliant field officers for the slightest reason, or for no reason at all.

Such meddling proved costly to Germany as well as to himself. The Second World War was so vast that one person couldn't master all the necessary details, which meant that he was bound to make mistakes—and mistakes in war are paid for in blood.

The strain of command gradually undermined Hitler's health. He lost his appetite and became listless from lack of sleep. Instead of consulting able doctors, he put himself into the hands of Dr. Theodor Morell, a quack who injected him with at least twenty-eight different drugs, including amphetamines, dangerous "uppers" that harmed him still more. To calm him down and allow him to sleep, Morell prescribed strong tranquilizers. Without a healthy diet or exercise and under the influence of powerful drugs, Hitler's health steadily deteriorated.

Stalingrad was the turning point in the Second World War. Before Stalingrad, the Germans believed they were the Master Race who'd conquer the world. The Allied peoples feared that this boast might, indeed, come true.

Stalingrad shattered German confidence. Entire towns went into mourning for their fallen sons. Newspapers were black with the little Iron Crosses that marked military death announcements. Millions of ordinary Germans began to doubt—*dared to doubt*—their Fuehrer's genius. Their cries of *Sieg Heil!* (Hail Victory!) took on a hollow ring.

Stalingrad gave the Allied peoples hope that the evil Hitler had unleashed upon the world could be eradicated. The road from Stalingrad was long and winding. It led across Russian steppes and North African deserts, over the Mediterranean Sea and the English Channel. But as surely as day follows night, it led to Berlin.

SLAVE EMPIRE

ADOLF HITLER WANTED A WORLD IN WHICH GERMANS WERE masters and everyone else their slaves. Despite defeats in Russia, he seemed to be getting his wish. By 1943, he'd conquered more of Europe than any dictator of the past. Not even the French Empire of Napoleon or the Roman Empire of the Caesars was the equal of Hitler's slave empire.

Der Fuehrer's plans for his empire were twofold: first rule, then exploit. If entire nations died as a result, that was all right with him, so long as they died serving Germany. He had no patience with talk of human rights. Only Germans had rights. They were the masters. They came first. Nobody else mattered. "Anyone who talks about cherishing [conquered peoples] goes straight to a concentration camp," he warned. Kindness was a crime in Hitler's eyes.

Step One: Rule.

As soon as new territories were conquered, they were put under control of fanatical Nazis like Reinhard Heydrich and Hans Frank, the governors of Czechoslovakia and Poland. These men took their orders straight from Hitler, obeying his every whim. They controlled the occupation forces, army units stationed in each country to prevent Allied invasion and rebellion. They also brought in the Gestapo to keep things running smoothly.

Everything came under Nazi control. Schools, newspapers, books, magazines, films, and the radio taught racism and obedience to *der Fuehrer*. Each citizen was issued a stack of papers—identification card, work permit, travel pass, ration book—that had to be carried at all times.

Anyone able to lead people against the Nazis was marked for death. In Eastern Europe, Gestapo teams began "housecleaning," a polite term for mass murder, as soon as possible. Government officials, army officers, teachers, priests, writers, scientists, and lawyers were rounded up and shot. Hitler's Night and Fog Order covered Western Europe. Those who might challenge Nazi rule there disappeared into "night and fog"—that is, they vanished without trace, and no information, not even their burial place, was given to their families. As in Germany, fear of the unknown helped Hitler to govern.

Step Two: Exploit.

Once a country came under tight control, it was looted. Everything useful or valuable was taken or bought with worthless occupation money, printed in Germany, which people were forced to accept in place of their own currency.

Thousands of tons of iron, coal, oil, wool, and timber were shipped to the Reich each year at no cost to the Germans. Factories were taken over and used to produce war materials. Dutch cheese, Danish butter, French wine, Polish cattle, Norwegian fish, and Russian grain poured into the Reich by the trainload.

Europe's artistic treasures were also stolen. Paintings, statuary, rare books, music manuscripts, antique furniture, carpets, and jewelry were carted off to the Reich. Most artworks went to German museums and libraries. The best items, however, wound up in Hitler's personal collection. Hermann Goering had so many famous paintings that there wasn't enough wall space to display them in his palace; hundreds had to be crated and stored in a salt mine.

Even common soldiers looted to their heart's content. German wives and sweethearts enjoyed the packages of perfume, lace, and silk stockings that came from occupied Europe. These were good times while they lasted. Few except those who received military death notices knew the true cost of their luxuries.

The Nazis stole people as well as property. Some human loot was to strengthen the "Aryan race" and replace men lost in the war. Experts from the SS Race Office went through occupied Europe to examine children, as stockbreeders examine cattle and pigs. Children thought to be of "good race" were taken away. If their parents objected, they were shot.

The youngest children were kept in SS orphanages and their names changed to prevent later identification. Kidnapped babies were given to German couples. Older boys were raised to become soldiers. Girls were educated to become mothers of future generations of soldiers. Children seen as unfit for soldiering or motherhood became slaves. It is believed that Hitler had 200,000 Polish children kidnapped, of whom fewer than 20,000 returned home after the war. The Germans call them "orphans of hate."

Germany's labor shortage grew worse each year. As the war spread, Hitler had to draft more and more men for the armed forces. But each additional soldier meant one worker less in a factory, mine, or field. Rather than fill these jobs with women, as the Allies were doing, he decided to use foreign slaves.

At least nine million slaves were brought to Germany during the war. Hitler would do anything to get the workers he needed—anything, that is, except pay them and treat them as human beings. Sections of cities were sealed off by the SS and every able-bodied person was rounded up. Church congregations and movie audiences were arrested. Villages were burned and their inhabitants taken away.

Slaves were meant to be used and *used up*. German factory owners who leased them from the government wanted the highest profit at the smallest expense. Their slaves lived in filthy barracks, ate watery soup or plain garbage, and wore sacks with holes cut for their arms and heads. At some plants French slaves lived in groups of five in dog kennels so small that they had to crawl in on all fours. These poor people were worked until they dropped. A bullet then made space for the next victim.

Although they'd turned Europe into a prison, the Germans found that belonging to the Master Race wasn't as pleasant, or safe, as their Fuehrer promised. Millions of people in the occupied countries refused to accept defeat and oppression. In their hearts and minds and spirits, they resolved to resist the invader.

People began to protest, to say "no" to Hitler. Most said it softly, so as to avoid trouble. They'd act stupid, pretending not to understand if a German asked directions. Or they sang patriotic songs and wore the national colors to show that they still cherished their country's independence.

Others protested violently. Secret groups known as the Resistance sprang up in every occupied country. Their aim was to hurt the slave masters in any way they could, paving the way for liberation by the Allied armies.

The Allies, especially the Americans and British, formed vast secret armies to aid the Resistance. The American OSS (Office of Strategic Services) and the British SOE (Special Operations Executive) were made up of experts in underground warfare. Each had its own schools to teach what agents needed to know: spying, radio communications, coding, sabotage, forging documents, burglary, assassination. Secret army laboratories produced devilish devices called "toys," such as miniature pistols and bombs disguised as lumps of coal to be shoveled into a ship's boiler. Secret army airplanes, speedboats, and submarines delivered agents and supplies to Resistance units in occupied Europe.

The secret armies and the Resistance made life miserable for the Germans. Each day, every day, trains were wrecked and electric power lines cut, time bombs were placed in cargo ships, and factory machinery was ruined with sand thrown into delicate working mechanisms.

Germans everywhere were fair game. Patrols were ambushed and the killers gone before help could arrive. Bombs exploded in mess halls, officers' clubs, and movie theaters used by off-duty troops. Officers riding in open cars ran into strands of piano wire stretched across roads at neck level; it was like running into a giant razor blade at fifty miles an hour.

Not even high officials escaped Resistance executioners. Hit squads cut down SS police chiefs in Warsaw and in Utrecht, the Netherlands. Killings often were carried out in broad daylight in crowded places to show that the Nazis weren't supermen, but could be reached anywhere. In certain cities the situation was so bad that Nazi leaders needed large police escorts just to cross the street.

The Resistance's highest-ranking victim was "Hangman" Heydrich. On the morning of May 27, 1942, the Czech Resistance bombed his car as he was being driven to his office in Prague. The Hangman died slowly, painfully, like so many of his victims.

The Fuehrer unleashed the SS and Gestapo against the Resistance. "The troops," said one Hitler order, "have the right and duty to use any means, even against women and children, provided they bring success."

This order was carried out to the letter. The penalty for hiding an Allied agent or Resistance fighter was death, not only for the "guilty" person, but for his family. Suspects were rounded up and tortured for information. Many died under torture and others went insane; few survived the war. The SS took hostages, threatening to shoot a hundred innocents to avenge a single German.

In Western Europe, as in Russia, towns were wiped out in reprisal raids. To avenge Hangman Heydrich, SS men massacred the people of Lidice, Czechoslovakia, and leveled

the town with bulldozers. In France, the Second SS Panzer
Division behaved like cowards and thugs. SS troopers packed
the citizens of Oradour-sur-Glane into the parish church
and burned them alive after a shootout with the Resistance.
Only seven people out of the town's eight hundred inhabitants escaped the massacre.

Hitler's methods backfired. Instead of making people give
up in fear, they deepened their hatred of Germany and
strengthened the Resistance. Violence brought reprisals,
which brought still more violence. Only Germany's defeat,
or the total destruction of the occupied countries, could
halt the slaughter.

Germany also had its Resistance; Nazi education and
Hitler Youth training didn't fool everyone. A few saw through
Hitler's Big Lie and kept themselves from being contami-
nated by it. That took courage and a willingness to risk
everything for the sake of truth and justice.

Outstanding among these were a brother and sister, Hans
and Sophie Scholl. Hans, born in 1918, was a medical
student in the University of Munich. Sophie, born in 1921,
studied biology at the same school. Only a short walk from
their classrooms were the main Nazi Party headquarters and
the beer halls where Hitler had gathered his first followers.

As teenagers, Hans and Sophie had joined the Hitler
Youth and the League of German Maidens. Doubts came
quickly. Hans resented the arrogant youth leaders and how
they bullied weaker boys. He couldn't see how learning to
shoot guns helped him toward his goal of saving lives as a
doctor. Sophie couldn't understand why Jews were so hated.
The Jews she knew were decent people, good neighbors,
and law-abiding citizens.

Both kept their doubts to themselves until 1942. As a medical student, Hans was required to spend a few weeks each year with the army at the front. It was there, in Russia, that he saw something that made his blood boil.

A group of women slaves, each wearing a yellow Star of David on her blouse, was repairing a road under armed guard. Among them was a thin, sickly girl swinging a heavy pick. Her face, once pretty, was gaunt, and her eyes showed such sadness that Hans almost cried. He reached into his knapsack and gave her a chocolate bar filled with fruit and nuts, a quick-energy food carried by all German soldiers.

She threw it on the ground. She hated it. She hated him. She hated everything German.

Hans drew back for a moment, for he'd never known such hatred. Then, pulling himself together, he picked up the chocolate bar and, plucking a wildflower from the roadside, placed them at her feet. "I only wanted to give you some pleasure," he said as he walked back to his train.

Hans turned only once, to find the chocolate bar gone and the flower in the girl's hair. He never saw her again, but that experience soon touched the lives of others.

Upon returning to Munich, Hans told Alexander Schmorell, another medical student, about the incident. They decided to do something to rouse the German people against Hitler. Late one night, when the streets were deserted, they set out with brushes and a can of green paint. On the main street, on the University wall, even in Odeon Square, they painted their message in letters three feet high:

DOWN WITH HITLER!
HITLER, MASS MURDERER!

And again and again FREIHEIT! FREIHEIT!—FREE-
DOM! FREEDOM!

In time, others joined them: Professor of Psychology Dr.
Kurt Huber, and medical students Christoph Probst and
Willi Graf. Sophie, however became her brother's closest
accomplice.

The little group called itself *die weisse Rose,* the White
Rose, because that flower is a symbol of cleanliness and
innocence. Hitler stood for the opposite, for ugliness and
guilt. The White Rose dedicated itself to rallying German
students against Hitler by writing leaflets telling the truth
about the Nazis and their crimes.

They knew the risks they'd be running. Detection would
cost them their lives. Yet they knew something else, something far more important: that to love one's country, really
to love it, means opposing it when it is wrong. What happened to them was unimportant. Germany alone counted.
Germany had to be cleansed of Hitler and his evil in order
to regain her dignity as a nation. "Traitor" is a harsh word,
and they were traitors according to Hitler's law. But theirs
was a noble treason.

Somehow the White Rose found a mimeograph machine, paper, and ink, which they kept hidden in Hans's
room. Although they shared the same ideals, Hans did most
of the writing. The first leaflet was finished by November
8, 1942, only days before the Russians sprang their trap at
Stalingrad.

Hear the White Rose.

Hitler, the leaflet said, was murdering the Jewish people
and destroying the soul of the German people. Hitler means
"the dictatorship of Evil." He must be crushed and his

"monster of a state" overthrown. People of goodwill must sabotage the war industries. No more innocents should die because of the lunatic in Berlin.

Four leaflets were issued that winter and distributed at great risk. Members of the White Rose took suitcases full of leaflets to other cities, where they were mailed to clergymen, students, and teachers, or left outside university classrooms.

The Nazis were shocked. For the first time opposition to Hitler's tyranny had broken into the open. And in Munich, the birthplace of Nazism! Heinrich Himmler ordered the Gestapo to cut off the White Rose at its roots.

The White Rose's fifth leaflet was ready by February 17, 1943, less than a month after the Stalingrad disaster. It was to be the last. Hans and Sophie were arrested the next day while throwing leaflets from atop the main staircase of the University of Munich. Although they claimed to have acted on their own, the Gestapo soon arrested their friends. All were tried for treason and beheaded by the public executioner.

After Sophie had been taken from her cell, a piece of paper was found on her cot. It was the death warrant. On the back of it, she'd scribbled a single word. The word was *Freiheit!*

The Nazis weren't allowed to forget the White Rose. Before the end of 1943, Allied bombers showered German cities with millions of their leaflets, copies of which had been smuggled out of the country by spies. Soon afterward, words were chalked on the walls and sidewalks of Munich in bold letters: DESPITE EVERYTHING, THEIR SPIRIT LIVES ON!

Hitler had carried a grudge against Jews since his days as a tramp in Vienna. As we've seen, he believed that Jews had ruined his artistic career and were an evil race bent on destroying his own "Aryan race." To prevent this, and to avenge his personal hurt, he decided to commit a crime unequaled in history.

That crime is known by different names. Hitler called it "the Final Solution of the Jewish Problem." To Jews it is the "Holocaust," the firestorm that nearly burned up their whole people. It was a crime so terrible that a new word had to be added to the English language to describe it. The word is "genocide," or the planned murder of entire peoples. Adolf Hitler wanted to murder every Jew in Europe—eleven million men, women, and children. He nearly succeeded.

Germany's 210,000 Jews learned Hitler was serious soon after he came to power in January 1933. Within days storm troopers were parading through Jewish neighborhoods, bawling songs of hate:

> When Jewish blood spurts from under the knife,
> Things will go twice as good as before.

Jews were fired from government jobs. Their houses of worship, or synagogues, were burned as police stood by doing nothing.

In 1935 Hitler issued the Nuremberg Laws on Citizenship and Race. No longer considered citizens, not even considered people, the Jews found their lives turned into a nightmare. Here is a short list of things Jews could not do or have in the Third Reich:

• Jews could not walk on certain streets, sit on park benches, use public swimming pools and transportation, visit mu-

seums, libraries, theaters, and movie houses, drive cars,
or have their hair cut by "Aryan" barbers.

- Jews were forbidden to own electrical appliances, radios,
typewriters, record players, or bicycles.
- In many places druggists refused to sell Jews medicines;
nor could they buy fruit or vegetables or even milk for
their babies.
- Jewish-owned businesses, farms, and shops were taken
away, along with most of the money they'd saved in banks.
- To make them easily identifiable, Jews had to wear a
yellow Star of David patch on their clothing with the word
Jude, Jew, in black letters. Jewish men had to take "Israel"
as their first name, Jewish women "Sara."

No wonder that by the late thirties the Jewish suicide rate
more than tripled as people lost hope. In 1938 one young
Jew's hopelessness brought desperate action. Crazed with
worry about his elderly parents, who'd been expelled from
Germany, he shot a diplomat at Hitler's Paris embassy. That
killing triggered the Crystal Night, or the Night of Broken
Glass, November 9–10.

On Hitler's orders, Hermann Goering and Reinhard Heydrich organized a reign or terror against the helpless people.
Synagogues went up in flames. Jewish stores were looted;
the remains of their plate glass windows littered the streets.
Thousands of Jewish men were dragged off to concentration
camps. The Jewish community was then forced to pay the
Nazis for the damage to their own property, plus a heavy
fine.

Jewish children felt the hatred as keenly as their elders.
They had been raised to think of themselves as Germans of
the Jewish faith; many of their fathers had served Germany

"ACHTUNG! PAPIER!" *Attention! Papers! Jewish men taken during a roundup in the Warsaw Ghetto have to have the proper identification papers or face immediate execution.*

and won medals during the First World War. Now they suddenly found themselves hated, shunned, spat upon.

Jewish boys and girls had to sit in class, listening attentively, while their teachers preached racism and told anti-Semitic "jokes." Play periods and after-school hours brought beatings from bands of Hitler Youth bullies. Complaining to a policeman or school principal might bring a slap or a curse like "dirty Jew." Finally, after the Crystal Night, all Jewish pupils were expelled from school.

Yet this was just the beginning. As long as Germany remained at peace, Jewish men might be killed in riots, but the lives of women and children were spared. With the world watching, *der Fuehrer* didn't dare commit mass murder.

The Second World War changed everything. Hitler's conquests in the East put the centers of Jewish life in Europe into his hands. Poland and occupied Russia alone had 5.5 million Jews, with another 1.2 million in Rumania and Hungary. The rest were scattered over Eastern and Western Europe and the Balkan countries. In July 1941, as the panzers rolled toward Moscow, Hitler decided to go ahead with the Final Solution.

Four Special Action Groups of about a thousand men each were formed and sent to the East. Each group was made up of SS troops and criminals released from prison for "special duty." Mission: follow the armies and wipe out Jewish communities behind the lines. Regular army commanders were to help them in any way possible.

A Special Action Group would round up all the Jews in an area and force them to dig a ditch in an out-of-the-way

place, such as a forest clearing. Next, everyone, young and
old alike, had to strip naked and place their clothes and
shoes in neat piles. Weather made no difference; naked
people were kept waiting in subzero temperatures. When
their turn came, the Jews had to go into the ditch and lie
down on the bodies already there. SS men with machine
guns and automatic pistols then shot them in the back of
the head.

In places like Babi Yar in the Ukraine, thousands of
people were mowed down each day. Here 35,000 died in
two days; eventually 100,000 bodies were buried in this deep
ravine. Altogether Special Action Groups murdered no fewer
than 700,000 Jews in less than a year.

Hitler wasn't satisfied. In January 1942, four months before his assassination, Hangman Heydrich was ordered to
draw up plans for murdering Europe's Jews quickly. Heydrich could take whatever manpower and resources he needed
for the Final Solution: building materials, railroad engines,
boxcars, police units. Militarily, the Final Solution made
no sense at all; indeed, it harmed Germany's war effort,
wasting manpower and resources. But that didn't matter to
Heydrich's master. Killing Jews had become as important
to Hitler as winning the war, perhaps more important.

Heydrich organized genocide like an assembly line, each
stage following the other in a logical order. He began by
building six camps in secluded areas of Poland near railroad
lines. Unlike concentration camps, where prisoners might
survive for years, these were extermination camps where
nearly everyone would be killed as soon as they arrived.
The camps were located at Chelmno, Belzek, Sobibor, Treblinka, and Majdanek. The name of the largest camp has

become a synonym for evil: Auschwitz. Although other peoples—Russians, Poles, gypsies—died in these camps, their main victims were Jews, regardless of their nationality.

In the meantime, sections of Polish cities had been set aside as ghettos. Ghettos originated in the Middle Ages as places where Jews were segregated from the rest of the community. Each ghetto was walled and had iron gates, which were locked at night, imprisoning the Jews. The old ghettos were prisons, but prisons where the inmates could build their synagogues, raise their families, and earn their living.

Heydrich's ghettos, however, were large holding pens where Jews awaited slaughter. Each was surrounded by walls topped with barbed-wire entanglements and broken glass set in cement. SS troops guarded the gates with machine guns. Poland's Jews crowded into these ghettos until their turn came to be shipped to the death camps. Jews from the rest of Europe usually went straight to the camps from their home countries.

Sooner or later Jews were rounded up and marched to a railroad station. There guards with leather whips and fierce dogs drove them into boxcars and locked the doors. The windowless boxcars were packed full; the only air came through cracks in the walls. There was no place to sit or go to the toilet. No food or water was given the doomed people, and many died before reaching their destination. Living and dead stood up, pressed against each other for days. As the trains came click-clacking down the tracks, bystanders along the way winced at the odor coming from the sealed boxcars.

The Jews were received at the camps by more guards and dogs, who drove them from the boxcars. The "selection" began.

The selection. Dr. Mengele, the "Angel of Death" (standing at left with cane), sorts new arrivals at Auschwitz into columns. The men on the right will become slave laborers. The women and children on the left will go immediately to the gas chambers.

An SS doctor pointed with a cane, directing each person to step into one of two columns. A handful of able-bodied men and women went to the right. Everyone else went to the left. The right-hand column would live a little longer; the left-hand column had only moments to live.

Loudspeakers blared instructions to those marked for death: "Strip, even artificial limbs and glasses. Hand in all money and valuables at the 'valuables' window. Women and girls are to have their hair cut at the barber's hut." The hair, mountains of it, baled and packed, was shipped to Germany to make insulation for submarines and mattresses for their crews.

Next came the dash along the Road to Heaven, the SS name for the long, narrow avenue bordered by fences of electrified barbed wire. At the end of the avenue was a low building. It was the Jews' last stop on earth.

Each camp had at least one such building. The killers had disguised it as a bathhouse in order to calm the Jews' fears so they'd go in without making trouble; sometimes loudspeakers played soothing lullabies. The building had several square rooms with cement floors, bare except for shower nozzles set every few feet in the ceiling. As many as two thousand people were packed into each "shower" room as tightly as possible; babies were handed in over the adults' heads. When the room was full, airtight doors swung shut and were locked. Then it happened.

An SS man on the roof opened a metal can containing about a gallon of dark blue crystals. This was Zyklon B, a chemical that became poison gas on contact with the air. The SS man, who always wore a gas mask and heavy rubber gloves, poured one can of crystals after another into a duct and screwed its lid back in place. The Jews suddenly realized that the "shower" room was a gas chamber when jets of choking, blinding vapor shot from the nozzles in the ceiling. All were dead within minutes, yellowed by the gas. The smaller camps could gas 6,000–8,000 people each day. Auschwitz was a death factory, claiming up to 15,000 victims daily.

The Nazis, being frugal people, "processed" the bodies into useful byproducts. Prisoners removed the bodies and opened their mouths; gold teeth were pulled out and the gold melted down for shipment to German banks. Tattooed skin might be peeled off, tanned, and made into lampshades. The bodies were then burned in outdoor pits or crematoria, great ovens that could consume hundreds of bodies each hour. Human fat was made into bars of soap. Human ashes were dumped into streams or used as fertilizer in vegetable gardens grown for the SS.

Those who'd been spared during the selection were worked to death on building projects near the camps. Thousands of others became human guinea pigs in so-called "medical experiments." Those who did these experiments were real-life Dr. Frankensteins, mad scientists with no respect for human life. Jews were not their only victims. Russian war prisoners, Polish women, gypsies, and children were also favored by Nazi doctors.

These doctors were very inquisitive. Any idea was tested immediately on defenseless people: high doses of X-rays, stuffing gunshot wounds with dirty rags, drinking sea water, experiments to see how much cold a person could endure and still be revived. To test new drugs, victims were injected with smallpox, cholera, and typhus germs. Those who didn't die painfully were shot or injected with gasoline at the end of the experiment.

Dr. Josef Mengele, chief medical officer at Auschwitz, earned his nickname of the Angel of Death. Mengele experimented with twins, trying to find ways of creating a race of blue-eyed Aryans in the laboratory. In the hope of turning brown eyes blue, he injected the eyes of one of a set of twins with dyes or poisons. Even the SS trembled in his presence.

Most of those who ran the death camps were ordinary people who believed they were doing the right thing. Racist education had poisoned their minds, making them see their victims not as fellow human beings, but as dangerous creatures that had to be exterminated. They saw themselves as loyal Germans duty-bound to obey orders—any orders. There was no question of personal responsibility for their actions. Orders were orders. If these were evil, that wasn't their fault, they believed, but the fault of their superiors. Thus one could do terrible things and still have a clear conscience.

When brought to trial after the war, nearly all Nazi killers pleaded innocent. Walter Rauff, who'd arranged transportation of Jews to death camps, explained, "There were terrible things done. . . . I'm not one who says he didn't know. I knew. But I was a soldier—right or wrong, my country. A soldier obeys. . . . I would do the same things again." Allied courts disagreed, and many Germans were hung as war criminals or given long jail terms.

If the Holocaust shows people at their worst, it also shows them at their best. Not all Germans were racists and murderers. Some, like the White Rose, refused to swallow Hitler's lies and risked their lives to help his victims.

Among them was Oskar Schindler, a wealthy factory owner

who risked everything to aid the defenseless. After the conquest of Poland, Schindler set up a metalware factory in the city of Cracow worked by Jewish slaves. Yet few slaves have ever been more grateful for their slavery. No one in his factory was ever beaten, let alone killed, but was treated with respect and decency. During SS roundups for Auschwitz, the "Schindler Jews" remained safe.

Oskar Schindler worked miracles. Soft-spoken and generous, he made friends easily. His best "friends" were high-ranking army officers and Gestapo chiefs, who were always welcome at his home and given valuable presents. They liked *"unser Oskar"*—"our Oskar"— and did him favors. Oskar used their friendship to save more than a thousand Jews. Jews hid in his factory during roundups. It was never searched, thanks to his powerful "friends."

Oskar even snatched people from the death trains. Learning that some of his workers had been arrested on the street, he drove to the railroad station. As Jews were being whipped into boxcars, he asked an SS lieutenant about his people. The lieutenant refused to release the Schindler Jews.

Politely, Oskar explained who he was and named his friends. The lieutenant shook his head; he had his orders and the Jews must go. "May I have your name," Oskar growled, pulling a notebook from his pocket. Then, dropping his voice, as if talking man to man, he made a promise: "I believe I can guarantee . . . that you'll be in southern Russia within a week." And Russia meant Stalingrad in 1942. Oskar's Jews were released on the spot.

Mostly, however, Jews had to rely on themselves. Those who could do so went into hiding to escape Hitler's bloodhounds. It wasn't easy. Some were able to bribe farmers to

allow them to live in pits dug under barns or sheds. Life
for these hunted people became a nightmare of fear, lice,
and oozing mud in a dark, foul-smelling hole.

In towns, Jews became "submarines," hiding wherever
they could find a safe place. One of these fugitives was Anne
Frank, a girl of thirteen who hid in a secret room above an
Amsterdam, the Netherlands, warehouse. Anne, her parents, and several friends lived in these cramped quarters for
two terror-filled years.

A sensitive girl, Anne kept a diary in which she recorded
her thoughts and feelings. Despite her ordeal, she never lost
faith in human goodness and in life. "In spite of everything,"
she wrote toward the end, "I believe that people are really
good at heart. I simply cannot build up my hopes on a
foundation consisting of confusion, misery, and death.
. . . Surely the time will come when we are people again,
and not just Jews."

That time never came for Anne Frank. Her family's hideout was raided by the Gestapo, and she was sent to a concentration camp, where she died.

Most Jews didn't fight back but went to their deaths without protest. The reasons for this were not cowardice or
stupidity. Far from it. Jews love life as much as anyone;
indeed, life is sacred in their religion. The only time Jews
may break God's sabbath is to save a life.

But they also loved their families. Jewish family ties were
very close. It was hard for a young, strong person to abandon
husband or wife, children, parents, and grandparents in
order to save oneself. As a result Jews often went to their
deaths as complete families.

There was something else. Hitler's plot was so monstrous

that Jews couldn't imagine such an evil possible. Nothing like it had ever happened before. As sane people, they assumed that Germans would act in their own best interests. Jews were useful as workers, even as slaves, in Germany's war effort. It made no sense to weaken that effort by killing so many useful people. Only later, when it was too late, did they understand that Hitler wanted them dead at whatever cost to his country.

Some Jews, however, fought back individually or as members of the Resistance. They fought less to save their lives than for revenge and for their self-respect. "Why did you kill a German?" Gestapo men asked a Jew on the gallows. "I hate you," he said. "I am sorry I killed only one German. I saw my parents killed in front of my eyes. In front of my eyes you killed ten thousand Jews." Then he cried, "Down with Hitler!" and spat in the hangman's face.

Jews fled the ghettos and joined the guerrillas in the forests of Poland and Russia. The Jewish Resistance extended into the death camps themselves. In Treblinka and Sobibor Jewish slaves attacked guards with tools and their bare hands. A few escaped to the forests; the others were killed. At Auschwitz Jews with stolen guns and grenades killed several guards and blew up one of the crematoria. The rebels were slaughtered.

The most famous revolt took place in the Warsaw Ghetto. When Hangman Heydrich set up the ghetto in 1940, a half million Jews were herded into it from all over Poland; the Jews themselves had to pay for building the walls that imprisoned them.

During the following years, thousands were arrested each month and sent to Treblinka. Disease and starvation took

hundreds of others each day. Children became so used to
seeing dead bodies in the streets, that they'd tickle them to
see if they'd move. A little girl named Martha wrote a poem
about her life in the Warsaw Ghetto:

> *I must be saving these days*
> *(I have no money to save),*
> *I must save health and strength,*
> *Enough to last me a long while. . . .*
> *I must be saving of tears that flow—*
> *I shall need them for a long, long while.*
> *I must save endurance these stormy days.*
> *There is so much I need in my life:*
> *Warmth of feeling and a kind heart—*
> *These things I lack; of these I must be saving!*
> *All these, the gifts of God,*
> *I wish to keep.*
> *How sad I should be*
> *If I lost them quickly.*

In July 1942, while the panzers drove toward Stalingrad,
about a thousand people set up the Jewish Combat Organization. Ways were found to leave the ghetto through
sewers to buy weapons from Polish smugglers. They were
able to gather a few dozen pistols, rifles, and hand grenades.
For the rest, their weapons were clubs, Molotov cocktails,
bottles of acid, and bare hands.

The ghetto's Jews, they knew, were doomed. Nothing
could save them. But the Jewish fighters pledged themselves
to kill as many Nazis as possible before dying in the ghetto's
ruins. The Germans had nearly cleared the ghetto by the
spring of 1943, when only 56,000 Jews remained within its

Exhausted after days of fighting without food or sleep, Jewish survivors of the Warsaw Ghetto uprising await their fate.

walls. Soon, the Nazis boasted, Warsaw would be "Jew-free."

April 19, 1943, was the first day of Passover, the holiday commemorating the Jews' escape from bondage in Egypt during biblical times. It is a holiday of freedom, and on that day the Jewish Combat Organization struck. German patrols ran into a hail of bullets and gasoline bombs. Some were killed, and their companions ran for their lives.

They ran! For the first time Jews saw SS troopers running *from them!*

Resistance in the Warsaw Ghetto lasted twenty-eight days. Seldom have people fought against such uneven odds. Jews, civilians without military training and weakened by hunger, fought the Weapons SS. SS General Juergen Stroop threw his forces into the battle. Planes, tanks, and artillery battered the ghetto. Troopers with dynamite and flamethrowers burned it house by house. Squads of Hitler Youth, brought especially from Germany, enjoyed the "thrill" of hunting Jews. They roamed the burning streets, eager to shoot anyone Jewish.

Occasionally they ran into more than they'd bargained for. General Stroop, who reported his progress to Berlin each day, was shocked that Jews preferred to be burned alive rather than surrender. Women fighters fired pistols with both hands. When captured, they waited for a German to begin searching them, then pulled a grenade from under their clothes, blowing themselves up with him.

On May 16 Stroop sent his final report: "The Warsaw Ghetto is no more." Its people were either dead or about to be killed at Treblinka. Its buildings were leveled to the ground.

Yet its people live on in memory. Jews have never forgotten the Warsaw Ghetto uprising. Each year, during Passover, they remember it in their prayers, along with the
flight from Egypt.

By 1945, some six million Jews had been murdered in cold
blood, victims of ignorance and race hatred. Adolf Hitler
had made good on his threat. His only regret was that he
hadn't been able to finish the task before his own time ran
out.

SMASHING THE THIRD REICH

EVERY WAR MUST END IN ONE OF TWO WAYS. ONE WAY IS through discussions in which the enemies compromise; neither side gets all it wants, nor does it lose everything. Another way is through force, with one side completely destroying the other's ability to resist. This was the way Adolf Hitler fought during his years of triumph. It was also the way the Allies decided to treat his Third Reich.

The Allied leaders—Roosevelt, Churchill, Stalin—believed that Nazi Germany was so evil that there could be no compromise with it. Their plan for victory may be likened to a gigantic wolf trap. The Russian jaw of the trap would close from the east, while the American and British jaw closed from the west and south. Between them, the Third Reich would be smashed to bits. Smashed completely. Smashed forever.

By 1943 the Allies had the means to carry out their plan. War industries in each country were running at full steam. Their output of planes, tanks, ships, and artillery outstripped Germany's by better than five to one. Allied planners could also count on the underground armies to keep Hitler off balance, forcing him to use precious manpower and resources to hold down the conquered peoples.

Still, nobody imagined that defeating Hitler would be easy. He might be insane, but he could read maps as well as anyone. He saw that for the Americans and British to get at him, they'd have to come across water. An invasion could come only across the English Channel from Great Britain or across the Mediterranean Sea from North Africa. The main blow, he believed, correctly, would come across the shortest distance, the twenty-one miles of water separating Great Britain from France. To prevent this, he created Fortress Europe.

Hitler put a million slaves to work on a line of steel and concrete forts along the French coast opposite Britain. Powerful guns were mounted in the forts and trained on the beaches. Underwater obstacles were planted to rip out the bottoms of landing craft. Beaches were sown with mines, barbed-wire entanglements, and machine-gun nests. Panzer divisions equipped with the new Tiger and Panther tanks, fifty-five- and forty-five-tonners, stood ready. Even if the Allies gained a toehold ashore, Hitler felt sure his panzers would sweep them back into the sea.

Fortress Europe, strong as it was, had a serious weakness. "Hitler," said President Roosevelt, "has built a wall around Europe, only he forgot to put a roof over it." At a conference in Casablanca, Morocco, early in 1943, Roosevelt and

Churchill gave orders for the Combined Bomber Offensive. American and British air fleets were to fly over the walls of Fortress Europe and tear out its insides with bombs. Germany was to be bombed "around the clock," given no rest day or night.

By day the United States Eighth Air Force, based in England, would go in for precision or "pinpoint" bombing, striking Hitler's war machine in its most sensitive parts. Heading its target lists were factories that made airplane parts, oil refineries, and communications: railways, bridges, tunnels, canals, power stations.

As the sun set and the Yanks headed home, RAF bombers would rumble through the gathering mists. The British specialized in "area bombing," marking out a large area of a city and blasting it completely. The idea was to keep German workers awake all night and make them homeless, forcing the Nazis to devote more energy to repairing damage than producing weapons. Hitler had sent the Luftwaffe against civilians early in the war; now the Allies would pay him back with interest.

Allied and German bombing forces were very different. Hitler had insisted upon two-engined aircraft to support the blitzkrieg. Light, fast, and poorly protected by machine guns, they carried small bomb loads to clear a path for the panzers. Had they been heavier, London might have been destroyed in the Blitz.

Allied bombers were built to fight their way through opposition and bomb cities. Planes like the American B-17 Flying Fortress and B-24 Liberator, and the British Lancaster and Sterling, bristled with machine guns in rotating turrets, enabling several planes to concentrate fire on enemy fighters. They needed four engines to lift heavy payloads and carry them long distances. Bombs came in sizes of 500, 1,000, and 2,000 pounds; 4,000-pounders were "blockbusters" able to destroy a city block. The Grand Slam was a 21,000-pound superblockbuster carried one to a plane.

Savage battles raged over Germany in 1943–1944. The Eighth Air Force hammered industrial cities such as Cologne, Mannheim, and Schweinfurt. Flying Fortresses visited the Messerschmitt works at Regensburg, causing serious damage. Once the "Mighty Eighth" hit its stride, it was able to put 3,800 bombers into the air each day.

Hitler's airmen fought bravely and well to protect their cities. Yank flyers called the routes to their targets the "blood highways of the air," for each raid cost them dearly in blood. From the moment they entered German airspace, they were hounded by fighters all the way to their targets, where antiaircraft batteries took over. The sky filled with the black puffs of exploding antiaircraft shells and the white streaks of tracer bullets. The wreckage of big bombers rained down, plowing the earth. Sometimes fully loaded planes, their controls shot away, crashed into towns. Crewmen plummeted earthward, trailing flaming parachutes. A 300-plane force might lose one fifth of its strength—60 planes, 600 men—on a single mission.

High losses continued until early 1944, when long-range fighters joined the American bomber formations. Bomber crews called the sleek P-51 Mustangs and the rugged P-47 Thunderbolts "Little Friends." Together they took control of Germany's skies from the Luftwaffe.

When Hitler came to power, he promised to make Germany's cities the grandest, most beautiful on earth. "Give me four years, and you won't recognize your cities," he'd boasted. By 1943 people were repeating his words as a sick joke. German cities *were* becoming unrecognizable, for on any given night 2,300 RAF bombers were turning them to ashes.

Germans still remember one RAF raid as *die Katastrophe*—the Catastrophe. The target was Hamburg, the Reich's largest city after Berlin. Hamburg lies along the Elbe River, near where it flows into the North Sea. A major seaport, it also built submarines and patrol craft; oil refineries and munitions factories lay along the Elbe and inside the city itself.

Hamburg had been hit several times by Americans in daylight raids. But the Catastrophe came in 1943, on the nights of July 24 and 25, when 700 Lancasters and Sterlings roared over the city in waves. The early waves dropped blockbusters to split open buildings, break water mains, and cut electrical cables buried under the streets. Later waves seeded the ruins with quick-burning incendiaries. These five-pound devils turned Hamburg into a furnace.

Thousands of fires blazed at once. There were so many of them, and they gave off so much heat that the Hamburg fire department was helpless. Gradually, the scattered fires joined, like oil spots spreading on water.

As the fires united, the heated air rose faster and faster, drawing in cooler air from the edges of the inferno. The cool air roared in with the force of a tornado. Trees were uprooted. Burning timbers and roof beams lanced through the air. Sparks leaped from one street to another. People were swept off their feet and hurled like missiles. The stronger the wind blew, the faster the fire spread and the hotter it became.

Hamburg experienced the first man-made "firestorm" in

history. A firestorm is just that: a storm of fire beyond human control. In Hamburg a wave of flame boiled along at temperatures of over 1000°, consuming everything in its path. Asphalt streets melted into a bubbling, sticky goo, then caught fire. Fleeing people were overtaken by waves of fire. Those who'd soaked their clothes in water to cool themselves were boiled alive as the water became steam. Anyone caught underground when the firestorm passed was burned as in a furnace; often all that remained were mounds of fine gray ash covering the shelter floors. When the firestorm burned itself out, 43,000 people were dead, hundreds of thousands homeless.

Panic swept the Third Reich. People in every large town began to mutter, "What happened in Hamburg can happen to us tomorrow." And it did.

Although few places had firestorms, bomb damage was dreadful. Berlin, visited by Allied bombers more than any other city, became a wasteland of craters and the skeletons of ruined buildings.

Hitler visited his ruined cities only once or twice; he never heard his people's cries or saw the fear in their eyes. As the war dragged on, Hitler lost contact with the German people. From 1942 onward, he rarely showed himself in public. There were no more speeches to frenzied crowds, no more rallies with a million people marching by torchlight and chanting his name. Once he could draw on the mood and passion of his audience to rally them to his side. Now he didn't *want* to know what the German people felt. He addressed them instead over the radio. His few speeches were flat, boring, nothing like those of the man who'd fought his way to power a decade earlier.

Hitler had little encouragement for the German people, and less for his soldiers. He even refused to see those wounded in his name. Once, when his private train stopped at a siding, he looked up to find eyes peering through the windows. A trainload of soldiers wounded in Russia had pulled up alongside, and the men, swathed in blood-stained bandages, were staring at him from their berths. Winston Churchill, even Joseph Stalin, would at least have waved. Not *der Fuehrer*. He ordered the windowshades drawn and kept drawn whenever troop trains were in the vicinity.

Whenever possible, Hitler spent his spare time at picnics and tea parties at the Mountain House, his home in the Bavarian Alps. He'd pass the hours reminiscing about past glories, dreaming impossible dreams for the future, and, as always, praising himself. While thousands of Germans went hungry, he swallowed chocolates filled with cherry syrup by the handful. As "the greatest German of all time," he felt he was entitled to such delicacies.

In the meantime, the Combined Bomber Offensive grew in fury and destructiveness. In 1942, the RAF dropped 48,000 tons of bombs on Germany; it joined the Eighth Air Force in dropping 207,000 tons in 1943 and a staggering 915,000 tons in 1944. Germany's cities were wrecked one by one and her armed forces deprived of vital war materials.

Yet the Allies paid a high price for their success. The air war against Germany cost the RAF 7,122 planes, plus 57,083 crewmen killed and 22,000 wounded. The United States lost 23,000 planes and suffered 120,000 casualties in battles over Fortress Europe.

The first step toward invading Fortress Europe was to drive Germany from the Mediterranean area. In the spring

Hitler with Eva Braun, at his retreat in the Bavarian Alps.

of 1941 Hitler had sent an army to aid Italian dictator Benito Mussolini in North Africa. That army, the *Afrika Korps*— Africa Corps—was commanded by General Erwin Rommel, the famed Desert Fox. Bold and cunning, Rommel was an honorable soldier serving an evil master. Unlike so many German generals, who cared nothing for prisoners' lives, he always treated captives well. Sometimes he gave dinners for captured British officers to explain their mistakes and tell what he'd have done in their place.

Rommel's mission was to cut the Suez Canal, Britain's lifeline to the oil fields of Iran and her empire in Asia. He began a desert blitzkrieg, driving across Egypt to a waterless spot in the desert seventy miles from the canal. The place is called El Alamein. There the Desert Fox met the Desert Rats, Britain's Eighth Army under General Bernard Law Montgomery.

"Monty," as his troops called him, had seen the horror of the trenches in the First World War. A calm, soft-spoken man who neither smoked nor drank, he valued his men's lives as his own. Never one to take unnecessary chances, he wouldn't move until he outnumbered and outgunned the enemy in every way.

Monty bided his time and built up his forces until October 13, 1942, when he began the Battle of El Alamein. That night the skirl of bagpipes drifted across the desert from the British lines. The Germans, shivering in their foxholes, knew that Monty's Scottish Highlanders were restless. And when they were restless—watch out!

Suddenly the eastern horizon went pink, and the bagpipes were drowned out by a terrific blast of gunfire. For six hours Monty's artillery blasted the Afrika Korps. Then, in the half-light before dawn, the gunners shortened the range and lay down a rolling barrage, a slow-moving wall of explosions. From behind the wall came the skirl of bagpipes and the clatter of tank treads.

The Desert Rats broke the German lines and kept going. During the weeks that followed, they pushed Rommel out of Egypt and into neighboring Libya. His veterans fought with their usual skill, but always with a strange feeling at the back of their necks. For somewhere behind them, to the west, were the Americans.

As the Battle of El Alamein raged, two task forces of American warships and transports sailed past the Rock of Gibraltar into the Mediterranean. Destination: the French colonies of Morocco and Algeria.

The task forces, one of which sailed directly from the United States, were commanded by General Dwight D. Eisenhower. "Ike" was an organizer who knew how to win people's trust and get them to work together. Although he'd never led troops in battle, he had a talent for picking able battle commanders.

The officers Ike chose would become famous throughout the Allied world; even the Nazis learned to respect them. Omar N. Bradley, with his white hair and thick eyeglasses, looked more like a college professor than a fighting general. But looks are deceiving, and Bradley was as tough as he was thoughtful. His friend, General George S. Patton, Jr., was his complete opposite. Hot-tempered and as quick to explode as a firecracker, "Old Blood and Guts" Patton was a cavalryman turned tank commander. Utterly fearless, he was always in the thick of the action with his two ivory-handled six-shooters. Patton had a knack for finding an enemy's weak point and lunging at it with all his armor. He had plenty to teach Hitler's generals about blitzkrieg.

The Yanks landed in Morocco and Algeria under an umbrella of naval gunfire on November 8, 1942. Pushing aside light resistance from French soldiers serving Hitler, they headed inland and began moving east. Rommel fought desperately, inflicting heavy losses on the Americans at the Kasserine Pass and elsewhere. But it was a losing battle. Low on supplies, especially fuel for his tanks, and caught between Ike's and Monty's forces, the Desert Fox escaped across the Mediterranean with the remnants of the Afrika Korps. Left behind were 350,000 German and Italian dead and prisoners. There were so many prisoners that thousands of them had to be sent to camps in the United States.

Victory in North Africa gave the Allies bases for invading Fortress Europe from the south. From Oran in Algeria to Alexandria in Egypt, and a dozen smaller seaports in between, Allied forces gathered in secrecy. Secrecy was important to safeguard their next operation, but it was more important as a preparation for the greater operation ahead.

It wasn't enough to keep Allied plans secret; the enemy had to be tricked into believing that the attack would come someplace else. Thus radio operators along the entire North African coast sent false messages in codes the Germans could easily break. Messages reported the fake movements of fake divisions to fake bases—*anything* to mislead the enemy.

In Operation Mincemeat the British dressed a corpse as a Royal Marine officer and gave it a briefcase with false papers. Corpse and briefcase were then put ashore in Spain, where the government was friendly to Hitler. Sure enough, the Spaniards passed the "information" to Nazi agents. The papers hinted at an Allied invasion of Greece, hundreds of miles east of the true target. Hitler fell for the trick and sent thousands of troops to surprise the invaders when they landed.

Der Fuehrer was surprised himself when the Allies stormed ashore in Sicily, July 10, 1943. For the next five weeks Patton's and Montgomery's forces drove Sicily's defenders from their positions. The Sicilian campaign cost the Germans and Italians 167,000 killed and wounded. Allied losses were 31,158.

Setbacks in North Africa and Sicily convinced some of Mussolini's key supporters that Italy was on the wrong side. Rather than see their country ruined, they tried to force him to give up control of the army and join the Allies. Had they succeeded, and had they let the Allies into Italy without an invasion battle, the war would have ended sooner, saving countless lives. Unfortunately, Nazi agents in Rome learned of the plot and Hitler acted quickly. Fresh German divisions joined those already in Italy and took over the country in a few days.

When the Allies landed in September 1943, they met some of the finest troops in Hitler's army. At Salerno south of Naples, and later at Anzio near Rome, the Yanks fought desperately for a beachhead. German artillery pounded the crowded landing areas. During lulls in the shelling, loudspeakers kept the GIs on edge with surrender demands in English: "Come on in and give up. You're covered."

Instead of surrendering, they attacked harder. Naval guns and dive-bombers laid down curtains of fire, allowing the GIs to move inland. Even so, nothing came easily in sunny Italy.

Italy's geography favored the defenders. Except for level areas along the coast, Italy is ribbed with mountain ranges that send rivers racing into the valleys below. This enabled the Germans to drag out the battle, making the Allies pay dearly for every gain. No sooner did the Allies clear them from one chain of defenses than they found them dug in behind the next ridge or river line. At last, after nine months of fighting, American troops captured Rome, June 4, 1944.

It was a glorious day. The Romans opened their hearts to the battle-weary GIs, some of whom were returning to the land of their fathers. Happy crowds filled the streets, waving homemade American flags. Pretty girls stuck flowers in the muzzles of the soldiers' rifles. Old men, tears streaming down their cheeks, offered GIs bottles of strong *vino*, wine.

The people of the Allied nations were thrilled at the fall of Rome. But what happened two days later took their breath away. American, British, and Canadian troops landed in France. The big push was on.

After North Africa, General Eisenhower took command of SHAEF, Supreme Headquarters Allied Expeditionary Force. SHAEF's mission was to plan and carry out Operation Overlord, the invasion of France from across the English Channel. The plan called for landing a hundred thousand men and their equipment on D-Day, the first day of the invasion. They were to come ashore on the beaches of Normandy, the coastal area of France along the English Channel. These beaches were the most heavily defended in Fortress Europe, and the enemy was expected to put up strong resistance.

But landing troops would be the easiest part. Once ashore,

the assault force had to be reinforced and supplied with six thousand tons of food, ammunition, and fuel each day. Since no large seaports were available, the invaders had to bring their own. Two artificial harbors called Mulberries were built of hollow concrete blocks, each the size of an eight-floor apartment house laid on its side. The blocks were to be floated across the Channel and sunk in the proper positions. PLUTO—Pipe Line Under the Ocean—was a wide plastic hose that would carry fuel from pumping stations in England to Normandy.

One thing worried Overlord's planners a great deal. North of Normandy, a day's march from the invasion beaches, the German Fifteenth Army was stationed at Calais, with a thousand tanks and self-propelled guns. Hitler kept this mass of armor under his personal control to be used only on his orders. The Fifteenth Army had to be kept away from Normandy at all costs, for if it moved before the invaders dug in securely, it might roll over the beachhead. Somehow *der Fuehrer* had to be made to believe the biggest lie of all, despite the evidence of his own eyes. He had to be convinced that the Normandy landings were a bluff and that the "real" invasion would come later, in the Calais area.

To do this the Allies created FUSAG, the First United States Army Group, under General Patton. FUSAG's bases were along England's southern coast, opposite Calais. When enemy observation planes were spotted, Spitfires rose to chase them away, but usually not before they had a good look around.

What they saw was reported to the Fuehrer. There were tent cities built for hundreds of thousands of troops. Tanks and trucks stood bumper to bumper in fields; planes were parked wingtip to wingtip along runways. FUSAG was aimed straight at Calais.

No, it wasn't. What Hitler didn't know was that his planes were being allowed to slip through the fighter screens. The Allies *wanted* him to know about FUSAG, for it was all a hoax. Its tent cities were empty, except for service troops to keep things in order. Its "vehicles" were rubber dummies that a mischievous child could have ruined with a hatpin. Its planes were of wood or outworn units unfit for further service. Only time would tell if Hitler believed in FUSAG.

In the early morning hours of Tuesday, June 6, 1944, American and British paratroops began dropping behind the German lines. Taking advantage of the darkness, they fanned out to capture bridges and road junctions near the invasion beaches. They were still fighting when dawn broke over the English Channel.

The German defenders rubbed their eyes in disbelief. But what they saw was real enough. The sea before them was covered with ships as far as the eye could see. More than five thousand ships stood offshore: battleships, cruisers, destroyers, torpedo boats, tugs, tankers, troop transports. All at once the warships' guns bellowed and roared. Overhead, the first of the 12,000 planes the Allies had gathered for D-Day appeared. The heavy bombers flew inland, searching out enemy targets. Dive-bombers and fighters blasted anything German that moved below. Far to the rear the French Resistance swung into action, ambushing relief columns and generally upsetting enemy preparations.

The first waves of assault boats reached the shore and lowered their ramps. Infantrymen swarmed onto the beaches.

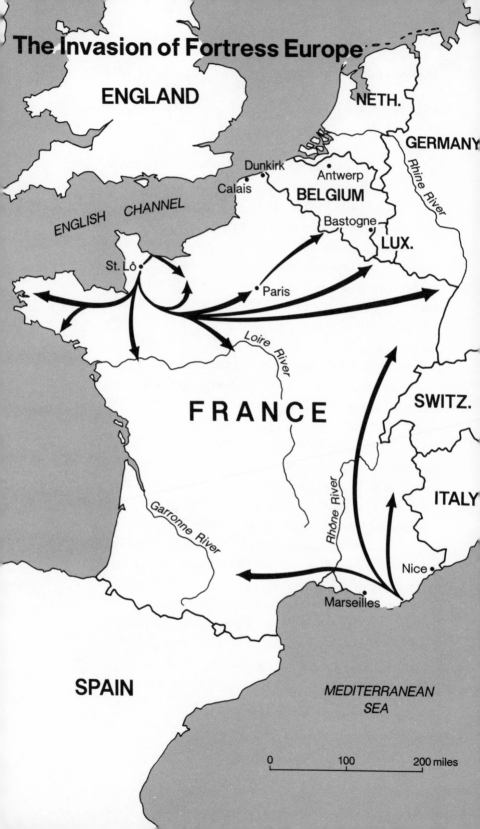

The Invasion of Fortress Europe

ENGLAND

NETH.

GERMANY

Dunkirk

Antwerp

Calais

BELGIUM

ENGLISH CHANNEL

Rhine River

Bastogne

LUX.

St. Lô

Paris

Loire River

FRANCE

SWITZ.

Rhône River

ITALY

Garronne River

Nice

Marseilles

SPAIN

MEDITERRANEAN SEA

0   100   200 miles

Many were seasick and vomiting, but they had to keep going or die.

The hardest fighting was at Omaha Beach—"Bloody Omaha." There American assault boats were blown to bits by mines and shells. The beach became strewn with dead and dying GIs, cut down by hidden machine gunners. "They're firing down our throats," an officer radioed his command ship anchored offshore. Another officer, Colonel George A. Taylor of the First Infantry Division, shouted, "Two kinds of men are going to stay on this beach, the dead and those who are going to die. Now let's get the hell out of here!"

That's just what they did. Slowly, painfully, paying with lives for every inch of beach, they made their way inland. By nightfall the Allies were ashore and digging in all along the Normandy coast.

And *der Fuehrer*? What did he do with his tank reserves? He did nothing. Ignoring pleas from his field commanders, he kept the panzers waiting near Calais for a whole week. FUSAG, the phantom army, had won a crucial battle without spilling a drop of blood.

Men and supplies poured into the beachhead after D-Day. By mid-July the Allies had over a million men ashore and were ready to begin the liberation of France.

The breakout began on July 25. On that day two thousand bombers soared over the German lines at St. Lô in the American sector. Explosives rained down, turning enemy positions into a moonscape of smoking bomb craters.

A flood of orders came from Fuehrer headquarters to hold St. Lô at any cost. They were meaningless, having nothing to do with the real world. When Panzer General

Fritz Bayerlein received one such order he replied, "Out in front everyone is holding on. Everyone. My grenadiers and my engineers and my tank crews—they're all holding their ground. Not a single man is leaving his post. Not one! They're lying in their foxholes mute and silent, for they are dead."

Hitler himself had narrowly escaped death a few days before the breakout. The White Rose was not the only Resistance group in Germany. There were also army officers, members even of the high command, who hoped to kill the tyrant.

Their leader was thirty-seven-year-old Lieutenant Colonel Count Claus Philip Schenk von Stauffenberg, a nobleman whose family had been fighting its country's battles for centuries. Stauffenberg was a handsome, gifted person who wrote poetry and loved music. He made friends easily, charming people with his warmth and gentleness.

Stauffenberg, like so many others, had welcomed Hitler's rise to power. *Der Fuehrer*, he believed, would make Germany strong and prosperous once again. He was proud to serve in the army.

That pride, however, turned to disgust when Hitler began his war of aggression. He came to see the Fuehrer as "a big nothing" who'd lead Germany to disaster unless men of conscience stopped him.

The year 1943 found Stauffenberg stationed in North Africa. While driving behind the lines one day, his staff car was machine-gunned by an American fighter. There was an explosion and everything went black.

When he awoke in a hospital days later, the left side of his face was bandaged. He could see no light through the

bandage, for his left eye was gone. Both arms were bandaged, and he couldn't move his left hand; it had been blown
off at the wrist. Two fingers were missing from his right
hand. He hurt all over.

Weeks in the hospital gave Stauffenberg time to think.
A deeply religious man, he'd lie on his back, trying to
understand why God had spared his life. Surely it wasn't
because he was someone special; better men than he were
dying every day at the front. If God spared him, it was for
a special purpose: to kill Adolf Hitler. "We must act," he'd
tell brother officers later, "for this man is evil incarnate."

Killing the Evil One wouldn't be easy. Hitler could send
millions of people to their deaths without batting an eyelash,
but he never took chances with his own safety. Whenever
he appeared in public, he wore a bulletproof vest under his
coat; a steel cap weighing three pounds was built into his
hat. To ruin a would-be assassin's plans, he'd announce a
visit to a certain place at a certain time, then change his
schedule without warning. Loyal SS guards surrounded him
always, making sure no one came near him with a gun.

Stauffenberg laid his plans carefully. When he recovered,
he found a post on the staff of the Replacement Army,
which sent fresh troops to combat units. As part of his job,
he had to prepare reports to be given to Hitler personally.
Sooner or later he'd come within striking distance of his
prey.

In the meantime, Stauffenberg persuaded friends, including several generals, to join his plot. Once Hitler was
dead, he'd use the Replacement Army to arrest the Nazi
leadership and put the Gestapo out of action. A new, democratic government would be formed to make peace with

the Allies. It was a daring plan that might cost the plotters their lives. But even failure would be a kind of success, proving to mankind that Germans were willing to risk everything to end the Hitler tyranny.

All was ready on July 20, 1944, when Stauffenberg was ordered to Fuehrer headquarters in eastern Germany. Before setting out, he stopped to pray alone in a Roman Catholic church in Berlin.

Late that morning Stauffenberg's plane landed at a secret airfield. From here he drove with an aide to the headquarters hidden in a forest surrounded by minefields and SS checkpoints. The guards examined their passes carefully, but not their briefcases. Each briefcase held a powerful bomb.

On the way to the conference room, the men stepped into an empty office, and Stauffenberg set his briefcase on the desk. Opening it, he grasped a pair of pliers with his three fingers and broke a glass vial. The vial contained acid that would eat through a wire attached to a spring, triggering the bomb in ten minutes. His aide's back-up bomb wouldn't be needed. Now there was no turning back.

Stauffenberg entered the conference room three minutes later. There he found Hitler and twenty-three others studying maps spread on a large oak table. The colonel saluted, clicking his heels. Hitler glanced at him, nodded, and turned away. There were seven minutes left.

A general was reporting about the Russian front, and Hitler was eager to learn the latest news. It wasn't good, said the general. The Red Army was advancing steadily into Nazi strongholds in Eastern Europe. If things continued this way, Stalin's legions would soon be in Germany. It was a moment of great danger for the Third Reich.

As the general spoke, Stauffenberg noticed that the table was resting on supports at either end, each a solid wall of wood. One support was only six feet to Hitler's right. "I'll leave my briefcase here. I've got to make a phone call," he whispered to Colonel Heinz Brandt. He put the briefcase against the support, left the room, and hurried out of the building to his car, where he joined his aide to await the explosion. In three minutes, if all went well, the bomb would tear off Hitler's legs, killing him instantly.

In the meantime, Colonel Brandt wanted a better view of the maps on the table. Finding the briefcase in the way of his legs, he moved it to the other side of the support, *away* from Hitler. It was the last thing Brandt ever did.

At exactly 12:42 P.M., a sheet of yellow light filled the room, followed by a blast that sent a shockwave bouncing off the walls. Suddenly two officers were lifted off their feet and flung headfirst through the windows. The oak table came apart in a burst of flaming splinters. The ceiling collapsed, pinning men beneath beams and plaster. Black smoke poured from the shattered building.

The explosion sent Stauffenberg on his way. In the confusion, he bluffed his way past the SS guards and boarded his plane for the flight back to Berlin. At last the tyrant was dead and the revolt could go ahead as planned.

He was wrong.

As rescuers ran toward the building, they saw Hitler staggering through the smoke. His trousers hung in shreds around his legs. His hair was singed, his right arm partially paralyzed, his eardrums punctured, and his backside a pincushion of splinters. But he was alive. Colonel's Brandt's moving of the briefcase had saved Hitler's life at the cost of his own;

three others died, two were badly wounded, and several had slight injuries.

Italian dictator Benito Mussolini arrived on an official visit soon after the explosion. Hitler, who'd once admired him as a model of what a dictator should be, now treated him as a servant who could be kept in power only by Nazi guns. Still, Mussolini was a good listener, who knew how to humor the Fuehrer. He'd never question or argue, only nod his head in agreement.

Hitler gave him a guided tour of the ruins, chattering all the while about his experience. Another person would have been frightened by such a narrow escape. Not Hitler! Being saved, he explained, was more than good luck, but a sign from Heaven that God wanted him to continue his work. He said:

> Look at my uniform! Look at my burns! When I reflect on all this, I must say that to me it is obvious that nothing is going to happen to me; undoubtedly it is my fate to continue on my way and to bring my task to completion. It is not the first time I have escaped death miraculously. First there were times in the first war, and during my political career there were a series of marvelous escapes. What happened here today is the climax! And now, having escaped death in such an extraordinary manner, I am more than ever convinced that the great cause I serve will be brought through its present perils and that everything can be brought to a good end.

To achieve that "good end," Hitler moved swiftly to crush the revolt. When he learned that Stauffenberg had left headquarters in a hurry, he ordered his arrest. By evening, loyal Nazis in Berlin were holding Stauffenberg and several accomplices at gunpoint. It was dark when they were hustled into the courtyard of the War Ministry and stood against a wall. The headlights of an armored car were switched on to give the firing squad a better view. Stauffenberg died shouting, "Long live our sacred Germany!"

Hitler's revenge was terrible. Nearly all the remaining plotters were hunted down by the Gestapo and tortured to reveal whatever they knew. About five thousand people were executed as a result of the July plot. The plotters' wives, children, and relatives, thousands of people, were sent to concentration camps.

Six generals were executed with a cruelty usually reserved for Jews in death camps. "It is my wish," Hitler told the executioner, "that they be hanged like cattle." And that's just what happened.

The condemned men were hung by the neck from butchers' meathooks with nooses of piano wire. They strangled slowly, twitching and kicking, while motion picture cameras recorded their agonies. *Der Fuehrer* had this horrible film shown again and again in his private quarters. He enjoyed every minute of it, although Dr. Goebbels turned pale and sat through the show with his hands over his eyes.

Hitler never recovered from his brush with death. From then on, his health grew steadily worse. His left arm trembled so violently that he had to hold it down with his right hand. His face became puffy and pale, and he sat hunched in his chair. Sleep became a luxury. As he lay awake at night, the scene of the flaming room flashed before his eyes, making his head reel. He may also have been suffering from

Parkinson's disease, a serious nervous disorder. All that the quack Dr. Morell could do for him was to inject more dangerous drugs.

Yet Hitler still ruled Germany. Armies obeyed his commands, even though millions knew that the war was lost. High-ranking officers, educated, able professionals, saw that most of his plans couldn't work—were, in fact, crazy. But they followed orders because of their loyalty oaths or out of fear for their own lives and the lives of their families. The SS and Gestapo spied on the military; the slightest hint of disloyalty, even in a top commander, brought instant arrest and death. Field Marshal Rommel, Germany's most admired war hero, was forced to swallow poison in order to save his wife and son. Where Hitler ruled, terror and murder ruled.

After St. Lô, the Allies broke out of the Normandy beachhead and, for good measure, invaded France along her Mediterranean coast. Patton, now leading the United States Third Army, sent armored spearheads lunging across France. Paris was liberated on August 25, 1944. Montgomery marched into the huge Belgian seaport of Antwerp early the next month. Hitler's forces were steadily being driven from the Netherlands and Luxembourg. Late in October the Yanks took Aachen, their first German city.

Der Fuehrer's armies were melting away. How would he use his last reserves? Where?

The answers were clear to the German high command. The reserves must go east to halt the Russians. If that meant defeat in the West, then so be it. Anything was better than being taken over by the "Communist savages."

An American armored car rolls under the Arch of Triumph during the liberation of Paris in 1944. The liberators didn't stay long, for immediately after the parade, they went into battle with Germans on the city's outskirts.

Hitler disagreed. With him it had to be all or nothing: Germany either won the war or perished. There was nothing in between. He'd gamble everything on one last campaign. It would be a repeat of the blitzkrieg of 1940, and it would lead to another Dunkirk, he predicted.

Hitler noticed on his maps that the American lines were thin in the Ardennes. GIs called the area the Ghost Front, because it was held by only four divisions sent there to rest after heavy fighting elsewhere. Nothing important ever happened along the Ghost Front. There were no artillery duels, no air strikes, no tank assaults. Both sides seemed to have forgotten about it.

Not Hitler. His plan was to break through the Ghost Front and take Antwerp, the Allies' main supply base for the Western Front. Once Antwerp fell, the Allies could easily be pushed into the sea, he insisted. The Americans, after all, were "bank clerks and Jewish hoodlums," not real fighting men. He was so blinded by hate that he couldn't see his enemy's strengths or his own weaknesses.

The generals objected to their Fuehrer's plan. They reminded him that the Allies were strong and growing stronger, especially in the air. It would take a miracle to break through in the Ardennes, let alone drive all the way to Antwerp. Hitler, who distrusted everyone since July 20, overruled them.

Preparations for Operation Watch on the Rhine went forward during the fall of 1944 in total secrecy. Trains came from every corner of Hitler's shrinking empire, bringing his last reserves to the target area. It was rough going, for travel had to be at night to avoid Allied bombers. Nearing the Ardennes, men and equipment moved over roads covered with straw to muffle the noise. By December, thirty divisions, 250,000 men, plus 2,000 heavy guns and 1,100 tanks, among them 70-ton King Tigers, lay hidden in the woods behind the Ghost Front.

The Americans suspected nothing. Christmas was near, and they looked forward to hot turkey dinners. For them the war was over. Germany was beaten. All they had to do was wait for General Eisenhower or Marshal Zhukov, the Russian commander, to finish the job in Berlin.

Saturday, December 16, 1944: Fog hung thick over the Ardennes. The Germans liked fog, and the thicker the better, for it grounded Allied airpower. German soldiers dressed in white camouflage suits waited under snow-covered trees. Tanks stood in lines along roads, waiting. As the luminous dials of watches came around to 5:30 A.M., artillery officers gave the signal.

"Fire!"

The barrage tore into the American lines. "Incoming mail!" GIs shouted as they dove into foxholes. The barrage roared for an hour, then stopped, giving way to an unnatural quietness. It was the lull before the storm.

All along the seventy-five-mile front giant searchlights were switched on and aimed skyward. Their beams reflected off the low clouds, creating a pale artificial moonlight. Ghostly forms clad in white stepped out of the forest gloom. Tanks rolled out of the haze, amid clouds of powdery snowflakes. The Battle of the Bulge had begun.

It is given that name because the Germans pushed a huge wedge, or bulge, into the American lines. Nothing was allowed to slow their advance. When 125 GIs were captured near Malmédy, Belgium, SS troopers marched them into a snowfield and opened fire with machine guns. The wounded, writhing in pain, were finished off with pistols.

The German attack continued unchecked for two days. One town after another fell to the tank columns. Nearly ten thousand GIs were trapped in the woods near Schoenberg and forced to surrender when they saw that rifles were useless against King Tigers. This was the largest surrender of American troops in Europe.

General Eisenhower, meanwhile, was rushing troops to the rescue. Paratroops of the 82nd Airborne and 101st Screaming Eagles divisions were sent to Bastogne, a vital crossroads in the path of the German advance. He also ordered Patton into the Battle of the Bulge with his Third Army.

Old Blood and Guts became the hero of the hour. "Patton! Patton!" people cried as his tanks roared through their towns. The general sped along icy roads in his jeep, shouting, encouraging, bullying the Third Army to move faster. Faster!

But Patton didn't rely only on soldiers and weapons. On December 22, he asked a chaplain to write a prayer begging God for a special favor:

PATTON: I want a prayer to stop this rain. If we got a couple of clear days, we could get in there and kill a couple of hundred thousand of those krauts.

CHAPLAIN: Well, sir, it's not exactly in the realm of theology to pray for something that would help to kill fellow men.

PATTON: What the hell are you—a theologian or an officer of the U.S. Third Army? I want that prayer.

Patton got his prayer; he had it printed and read to his troops, along with his Christmas greetings.

The Germans had surrounded Bastogne that very morning, and its defenders needed a miracle. Tanks and artillery were tearing it apart when some Germans appeared under a flag of truce. Their leader, a major, had a message for Bastogne's commander, Brigadier General Anthony C. McAuliffe of the 101st Airborne. The message was a demand that he surrender or have his command wiped out.

McAuliffe's reply was brought to the waiting Germans. It was short and sweet: "To the German commander—NUTS!—the American commander."

"But what does it mean?" asked the German major.

"In plain English," replied one of McAuliffe's aides, "it's the same as 'Go to Hell.' And I'll tell you something else. If you continue to attack, we'll kill every goddamn German that tries to break into the city. . . . On your way, Bud." *That* the major understood.

The Yanks had their miracle the next morning, December 23. Dawn came to the Ardennes clear and bright. "Hot dog!" cried Patton. "I guess I'll have another hundred thousand of those prayers printed. The Lord is on our side, and we've got to keep Him informed about what we need." He had the chaplain brought to his quarters and gave him a medal on the spot.

Airpower decided the Battle of the Bulge. The Americans owned the sky over the Ardennes. With shrieking engines, P-47s darted overhead. Now the GIs understood why pilots called them Thunderbolts. They'd come in at treetop level, machine-gunning enemy troops and pumping rockets into Tiger tanks. The explosions were music to the infantrymen's ears.

Cargo planes appeared in V-formations, one behind the other, to fill the sky with colorful supply parachutes. GIs shouted and danced and hugged each other in the streets of Bastogne. Patton's tanks drove into town a few days later. With Patton's Third Army advancing from the south and the United States First Army driving down from the north, the German position was hopeless. Although fighting dragged on for another month, Hitler had lost his gamble. The Battle of the Bulge broke his forces in the West. Left behind were 120,000 German dead and prisoners; over 600 tanks were burned-out shells. Broken also was the spirit of the German soldiers. Those who survived the Bulge knew that the Third Reich was doomed.

The Yanks had paid a fearful price for their carelessness and their victory: 76,890 killed, wounded, and missing. But they had proven themselves better than the Nazi "supermen."

The New Year, 1945, found Hitler's forces retreating everywhere. In the West, Allied armies crossed the Rhine River and stabbed into the German heartland. Air attacks gradually slackened off as the bombers ran out of worthwhile targets. The last big raid of the war was against Dresden, a communications center for the Eastern Front. On February 13–14, American and British planes fire-bombed Dresden, killing 135,000 people in the bloodiest air raid in European history. The Russians, meanwhile, knocked Hitler's allies Finland, Hungary, and Rumania out of the war. Red Army tanks rolled across Poland and into the Reich itself. Patton's tanks broke into Czechoslovakia.

Hitler continued to direct his war. He gave impossible orders, even to divisions that had been wiped out weeks before. When his plans failed, he ranted and raved about the soldiers' "stupidity" and "cowardice." When the Adolf Hitler SS Division retreated before the Russians, he demanded that they turn in their armbands as a punishment. That was too much even for the SS; some troopers sent *der Fuehrer* an armband still wrapped around the arm of a slain comrade. Staff officers kept it from him for fear of another temper tantrum.

The Allies advanced, but along with the joy of victory came sobering sights. Allied troops soon came upon the hells Hitler had created for "racial inferiors." Soviet troops were stunned when they overran Auschwitz and the other death camps in Poland. Men who thought they'd seen everything there was to see of war's horrors realized that they hadn't seen anything. Veterans of Stalingrad and a hundred other battles cried in front of mounds of unburied bodies and warehouses full of hair, eyeglasses, and shoes—*children's* shoes.

It was the same with the Americans and British. Late in April 1945, they swept into the Belsen, Buchenwald, and Dachau concentration camps. A young GI from Portland, Maine, wrote his wife from Buchenwald:

> Today there are still a few thousand left not by any show of humaneness or mercy on the part of the SS killers, but rather due to the sudden advent of our combat units which overran these places with such speed as to preclude the extinction of such life as was left to these unfortunates. I say some thousands are still alive, but some would be better dead. Too weak even to move, they lie with glazed eyes unable to move their emaciated bodies. . . .

We saw piled up stacks of bodies with twitching
limbs . . . —piles of white ash with pieces of un-
burned bone protruding—spick and span cremato-
riums—immaculate execution chambers. . . . It was
said that here experiments were conducted on toxic
gases, using human guinea pigs. Altogether possible
since in one room I saw organs of the body floating
in jars dispersed along shelves—here a brain, there
a liver. . . .

The camps were usually liberated easily, because the SS
guards, brave enough against helpless prisoners, didn't want
to tangle with Allied soldiers. Only at Dachau did the SS
put up a fight.

GIs arrived at Dachau in the afternoon of April 29, 1945.
It was a madhouse. Inmates poured out of their barracks,
living skeletons who knew their ordeal was about to end.
Bumping into each other, stumbling, picking themselves
up, they ran to welcome their liberators. *"Amerika gut!"*
cried a toothless man with bulging eyes and hollow cheeks.
"Amerika sehr gut!" "America is good! America is very good!"

Just then SS men opened fire from the watchtowers with
machine guns. That was a mistake.

Jeeps with machine guns mounted on tripods screeched
to a stop. Streams of hot lead stitched the watchtowers. Few
SS men were allowed to surrender. As they came out from
behind their weapons, their hands half-raised or perhaps
fully raised, the GIs shot them down. Corpses of SS men
were thrown from the watchtowers. Each time a Nazi hit
the ground, the inmates cheered.

Soon Dachau was secure. The place was a hellhole with

the dead and dying everywhere. The more the GIs saw, the angrier they became. They hated the SS as much as the camp's inmates.

Their hatred caught fire when a group of 125 guards was marched in at gunpoint and told to wait near a wall. These SS men were clean and well-fed. Arrogant even in defeat, they seemed proud of what they'd done.

"I'd like to kill 'em with my bare hands," a GI muttered.

"Kill 'em! Kill 'em! Kill 'em!" the others chimed in.

Then they lost control. Instead of behaving as disciplined soldiers, they became an armed mob. The SS men were shot where they stood.

It is a crime to shoot prisoners of war. But the GIs who'd done the shooting had seen such terrible things that day that their feelings ran away with their good sense. Although everyone knew who'd pulled the triggers, no one ever stood trial.

The end of Nazi Germany was drawing near. A week before Dachau's liberation, on April 21, Russian troops surrounded Berlin, trapping Hitler. He could have escaped, but chose to die in his capital.

Death was now all he could think about, his own death and that of the German nation. After surviving Stauffenberg's bomb he'd said, "I am beginning to doubt whether the German people is worthy of my ideals." Germany had let him down. Germany, therefore, must die. He ordered that everything valuable—cities, food supplies, factories, dams, museums, bridges—be dynamited. The victorious Allies must find themselves in a vast graveyard. Luckily, the Allies moved too fast for this plan to be carried out.

Hitler spent his last week of life like a creature of darkness that shuns the clean light of day. He lived in a deep shelter, or bunker, beneath the Reich Chancellery garden. It was an eerie world of gloom and dampness and noise. Although the sounds of battle seldom penetrated the bunker's thirty feet of concrete, Hitler was constantly shouting. Wild-eyed, with flecks of spittle in the corners of his mouth, he'd shout at the top of his voice. Traitors, bunglers, idiots, Communists, Jews—he blamed everyone but himself for the disaster. Only *der Fuehrer* was great and good and wise.

Above ground, Berlin was an inferno. Russian artillery and planes pounded it without letup. Fires blazed everywhere. Dust and ash swirled through the streets. Animals, their zoo cages broken open, ran about in terror.

Berlin's defenders, mostly old men of the Home Guard and scrawny Hitler Youths, were outnumbered ten to one by the Russian veterans. House by house, street by street, the Red Army smashed its way toward the city's center. Russian machine gunners scaled the Brandenburg Gate to take cover behind the Goddess of Victory and her chariot.

On April 29, as the Yanks stormed Dachau, Russian patrols came to within a block of the Reich Chancellery. Early that morning, Hitler married Eva Braun, his long-time companion. It was not a joyful occasion, for the newlyweds knew they'd reached the end of the line.

The next day, April 30, they said their goodbyes and went into Hitler's private apartment. Eva sat on the couch and swallowed poison. Her husband put a pistol to his head and pulled the trigger.

SS guards wrapped the bodies in blankets and carried them into the Chancellery garden. Shells were bursting

Hitler's last soldiers. Teenage members of the Hitler Youth were rushed to the front to halt the Russian armies advancing on Berlin.

nearby. Bullets popped overhead. They put the bodies into a shell hole, poured gasoline over them, and threw in a lit match.

Hitler's closest henchmen shared his fate. The day after his death, Dr. Goebbels poisoned his six children and then had an SS man shoot him and his wife; their bodies were also burned in the Chancellery garden. SS chief Himmler took poison when arrested by British troops. Hundreds of officers shot themselves rather than face capture; families of Nazi officials, including children, took poison.

In 1946 leading Nazis were put on trial as war criminals by an international court at Nuremberg; hundreds of lower-ranking officials and soldiers were tried by military courts. Many were executed for their crimes or given long jail sentences. Hermann Goering, however, cheated the hangman by taking poison.

Some officers escaped altogether. Dr. Josef Mengele, the Angel of Death, fled to South America, where he drowned accidentally in 1979. Other Nazi war criminals may still be free today.

Adolf Hitler's legacy is part of our world today. We cannot escape it.

Part of that legacy is a broken nation. Because of Hitler, Germany is divided and will probably remain so for generations to come.

Another, more important, part of the Hitler legacy is a warning and a lesson. The warning is that although democracy is still the best form of government, it can be quickly destroyed; we must never take it for granted. The lesson of Hitler is that people guided by hatred and unreason are capable of any and all crimes.

It is right that the last word on Adolf Hitler should come from a memorial to his victims. At a cemetery outside Leningrad, nearly one million victims of the siege lie buried in common graves. It is never without visitors, who pause to read a two-line inscription carved in the cemetery wall:

> Let no one forget;
> Let nothing be forgotten.

Remembrance. Yes, that is surely the greatest lesson to be learned from the tyrant's life.

SOME MORE BOOKS

There are thousands of books on Adolf Hitler, his Third Reich, and the Second World War. Here are some of the books I found most helpful in preparing this one.

Abel, Theodore. *Why Hitler Came to Power.* New York: Prentice-Hall, 1938.

Baldwin, Hanson W. *The Crucial Years, 1939–1941.* New York: Harper & Row, 1976.

Bauer, Yehuda. *A History of the Holocaust.* New York: Franklin Watts, 1982.

Bullock, Alan. *Hitler: A Study in Tyranny.* London: Odhams, 1964.

Calic, Édouard. *Reinhard Heydrich.* New York: William Morrow, 1982.

Clark, Alan. *BARBAROSSA: The Russian-German Conflict, 1941–45.* New York: William Morrow, 1965.

Craig, William. *Enemy at the Gates: The Battle of Stalingrad.* New York: E. P. Dutton, 1973.

Deighton, Len. *Battle of Britain.* New York: Coward, McCann & Geohegan, 1980.

———. *Blitzkrieg: From the Rise of Hitler to the Fall of Dunkirk.* New York: Knopf, 1980.

Downing, David. *The Devil's Virtuosos: German Generals at War, 1940–1945.* New York: St. Martin's Press, 1977.

Feig, Konnilyn G. *Hitler's Death Camps.* New York: Holmes & Meier, 1979.

Frank, Anne. *The Diary of a Young Girl.* Many editions and publishers.

Grunberger, Richard. *The 12-Year Reich: A Social History of Nazi Germany, 1933–1945.* New York: Holt, Rinehart and Winston, 1971.

Hanser, Richard. *A Noble Treason: The Revolt of the Munich Students Against Hitler.* New York: G. P. Putnam, 1979.

Infield, Glenn B. *Hitler's Secret Life.* New York: Stein & Day, 1979.

Jenks, William A. *Vienna and the Young Hitler.* New York: Columbia University Press, 1960.

Keneally, Thomas. *Schindler's List.* New York: Simon & Schuster, 1982.

Kubizek, August. *The Young Hitler I Knew.* Boston: Houghton Mifflin, 1955.

Lord, Walter. *The Miracle of Dunkirk.* New York: Viking Press, 1982.

Manvell, Roger, and Heinrich Fraenkel. *Himmler.* New York: Putnam, 1965.

——. *The Men Who Tried to Kill Hitler.* New York: Coward-McCann, 1964.

Mason, Herbert Molloy, Jr. *To Kill the Devil.* New York: W. W. Norton, 1978.

Middlebrook, Martin. *The Battle of Hamburg.* New York: Charles Scribner, 1980.

Mosse, George L. *Nazi Culture.* New York: Grosset & Dunlap, 1965.

Payne, Robert. *The Life and Death of Adolf Hitler.* New York: Praeger, 1973.

Salisbury, Harrison E. *The 900 Days: The Siege of Leningrad.* New York: Harper & Row, 1969.

Selzer, Michael. *Deliverance Day: The Last Hours of Dachau.* Philadelphia: J. B. Lippincott, 1978.

Seth, Ronald. *Stalingrad.* New York: Coward-McCann, 1956.

Shirer, William L. *The Rise and Fall of the Third Reich.* New York: Random House, 1970.

Snyder, Louis L. *Encyclopedia of the Third Reich.* New York: McGraw-Hill, 1976.

Terraine, John. *A Time for Courage: The Royal Air Force in the European War, 1939–1945.* New York: Macmillan, 1985.

Toland, John. *Battle: The Story of the Bulge.* New York: Random House, 1959.

Vogt, Hannah. *The Burden of Guilt: A Short History of Germany, 1914–1945.* New York: Oxford University Press, 1964.

Waite, Robert G. L. *The Psychopathic God: Adolf Hitler.* New York: Basic Books, 1977.

Werth, Alexander. *Russia at War, 1941–1945.* New York: E. P. Dutton, 1964.

Zeller, Eberhard. *The Flame of Freedom: The German Struggle Against Hitler.* London: Oswald Wolff, 1967.

Ziemer, Gregor. *Education for Death.* New York: Oxford University Press, 1941.

Zeman, Z. *Heckling Hitler: Caricatures of the Third Reich.* London: Orbis, 1984.

INDEX